Dynamic Studies in Hebrews

Bringing God's Word to Life

Fred A. Scheeren

WestBow
PRESS

A DIVISION OF THOMAS NELSON
& ZONDERVAN

Scripture taken from the King James Version of the Bible.
Scripture quotations taken from the Holy Bible, New Living Translation, Copyright © 1996, 2004. Used by permission of Tyndale House Publishers, Inc., Wheaton, Illinois 60189. All rights reserved.

WestBow Press books may be ordered through booksellers or by contacting:

WestBow Press
A Division of Thomas Nelson & Zondervan
1663 Liberty Drive
Bloomington, IN 47403
www.westbowpress.com
1 (866) 928-1240

ISBN: 978-1-4908-3806-9 (sc)
ISBN: 978-1-4908-3807-6 (e)

Library of Congress Control Number: 2014909428

Printed in the United States of America.

WestBow Press rev. date: 06/25/2014

DEDICATION

I WISH TO dedicate this book to my lovely wife, Sally, who is a Jewish believer. She has stood by me over the years and raised our sons in our God-loving home. The comfort of sharing our friendship and our love for Christ has encouraged me greatly in creating this series of dynamic studies of various books of the Bible. Sally's participation in our small group studies has added a much deeper dimension of richness to the discussions as a result of her sharing her heritage, training, and knowledge.

Contents

ACKNOWLEDGMENTS

MY FRIEND, BOB Mason, when in his second career as the Pastor of Small Groups at the Bible Chapel in the South Hills of Pittsburgh, suggested the overall structure of each study session. Realizing our group was doing more in-depth work than most, he asked that I include several important segments in each session: most specifically, the warm-up phase and the life application phase.

One great resource for this, suggested by Bob, is the New Testament Lesson Planner from InterVarsity Press. I have augmented this with commentaries by Chuck Missler from Koinonia House, the Wiersbe Bible Commentary, and the whole of Scripture itself. To make the utilization of the whole of Scripture more efficient, I have also leaned heavily on the Libronix Digital Library, perhaps the most advanced Bible software available. I have also utilized a number of other resources to help us understand how the New Testament and the Tanakh (Old Testament) fit together as one cohesive document.

During the course of preparing *Dynamic Studies in Hebrews*, it has been my privilege to collaborate with my friend, Rabbi Jeff Kipp. I found out that Jeff was delivering a series of lessons on this mysterious book at the same time as me. I asked him if he'd be willing to share his notes because his background in Judaism and the Old Testament Scriptures adds just what one needs to better understand this book.

I should also add a quick summary of Jeff's life. Over 30 years ago, Jeff was an adventuresome and skeptical young Jewish man whose life was a mess. He was a heroin addict who had been in and out of jail at least four times. In 1973 Jeff met Yeshua Ha-Mashiach, the Jewish Messiah we know as Jesus Christ, on a personal basis and his life turned around.

Shortly thereafter his wife, Cathy, was attacked by a knife-wielding assailant who stabbed her 15 times. Miraculously, the attacker missed hitting any of Cathy's vital organs and she fully recovered from the attack. As a result of this second miracle (the first having occurred when Jeff came to trust in Yeshua) Jeff's family also came to faith.

Jeff's life has been like that ever since he became a believer. His life is better, meaningful, fulfilling, and at the same time, more difficult. He leads a Messianic Jewish congregation and is on the staff of Chosen People Ministries. His in-depth knowledge of the Scriptures and his gift of passionately explaining God's Word have made him a popular speaker across the United States.

Jeff's gifts and knowledge were fully in evidence when I sent him an e-mail on a Saturday in 2011 after the President of the United States delivered a speech abandoning Israel. I wanted to talk with him about this event as it related to prophecy. He called me on the way to the Shabbat services he was leading and I felt like I was talking to Isaiah or some other famous personage from the Old Testament. I had already researched the text about these events and was anxious to compare notes with Jeff. He amazed me by ripping off just about every Old Testament reference to this time in prophecy and history by memory. He is a great Rabbi, a true brother, and a valued friend.

In addition to Jeff, I am grateful to all of the people in our small group Bible study with whom I first used this material. This fine group of diverse people has grown closer together as a result of our regular meetings and we have seen some miraculous things happen in each other's lives.

Our members included:

- Cathy Harvey, a high school teacher and dog breeder who was healed of a serious eye disorder during the course of our studies

- Dr. David Fink, a former pastor and professor of Greek

- Joyce Smith Fink, former assistant to the President at Pittsburgh Theological Seminary

- Scott Swart, former marine with a White House security clearance currently involved with the Washington City Mission and who holds a degree in theology

- Wendy Swart, a business owner and operator

- Ron Carrola, a well-known transportation engineer

- Felicia Carrola, who was fully engaged homeschooling her several children, one of whom was composing full orchestral scores and another who published a book while still in high school

- Tom Nicastro, the local service manager for a major international corporation

- Cindy Nicastro, a physical therapist with many years of expertise and experience and who proved to be one of the best of the best when she worked with me during my recovery from a recent hip replacement

- My wife Sally, an attorney in private practice, whose Jewish brother, a successful real estate developer, became a believer during the course of our studies in the book of Romans

- Barbara Thompson, Past Chairman of the Board of the Obesity Action Coalition, noted author and speaker, and currently Chairman of the Department of Library and learning resources at the Community College of Allegheny County's North Campus

- Frank Thompson, Retired Air Force Master Sargeant and currently Vice President and Manager of the WLS Center

Of course, having read the roster of the people in this particular small group, you may be wondering how you could *not* have a great Bible study with so many well-read, intelligent, and successful people in it. The mix of people, of course, is no accident. God's plan is greater than any we can imagine. His caring for us certainly includes the makeup of any small group devoted to the study of His Word. I believe every such small group convened for this purpose will have a mix of participants similarly suited to enhance the growth and learning of the group members individually and the group as a whole.

I believe you will find going through this material enjoyable and helpful, and you will likely find it more enjoyable if you have the privilege of going through it with a small group of believers, as I have been privileged to do. I know I feel as though I have gotten more out of the study than I would have if I had studied all by myself.

Speaking of small groups, Chuck Missler, a former Fortune 500 CEO, claims this is where he experienced the greatest growth in his life as a believer. I believe you may find this to be true in your experience, and I encourage you to be an active participant in such a mutually supportive, biblically based group.

May God bless you, inspire you, teach you, and change your life for the better as you go through these sessions.

IN SOME WAYS, the book of Hebrews is best studied as part of a trilogy. This relates specifically to one very important verse from the Old Testament. In particular, we should take a look at Habakkuk 2:4 which says:

"Look at the proud! They trust in themselves, and their lives are crooked. But the righteous will live by their faith." (NLT)

Or in the King James Version:

"Behold the proud, His soul is not upright in him; But the just shall live by his faith."

This could be said to tie directly into the New Testament books of Romans, Galatians, and Hebrews.

The book of Romans tells us who is considered just or righteous.

The book of Galatians tells us how they shall live.

The book of Hebrews teaches us about the faith and obedience of these people.

With this perspective, one can gain a better appreciation of the book of Hebrews. By reading it together with the New Testament books of Galatians and Romans, we gain a very good foundation in many of the basics of what is demonstrably the Word of God.

INTRODUCTION:
GROUND RULES

I DESIGNED THE first portion of each study to encourage everyone to think about their personal situation and get them involved. I designed the second portion to help people understand what the text says and how it relates to the whole of Scripture. And finally, each session ends with a discussion designed to help those present apply that day's lesson to their lives.

You will notice that, in most instances, I have included the citation, but not the actual text of the portion of Scripture that we are considering. I did this on purpose. I believe we all learn more effectively if we have to dig out the text itself. As a byproduct of that exercise, we all become more familiar with this marvelous book.

You will also notice the Scripture references are preceded by or followed by a question or series of questions. Again, I did this on purpose. I have also found that people seem to learn most effectively when employing the "Socratic Method." That is, instead of telling someone what the text says and how it relates to other texts and life, they will remember it much more completely if they answer questions about it and ferret out the information for themselves.

In a few instances, I have inserted additional commentary or partial answers to some of the questions to help the group get the greatest possible good out of the study.

In addition, I have added various Scriptural references, intending that they be read out loud as part of the session. Shorter passages might be read by one participant, while anything over two or three verses might serve everyone better if one member reads one verse and another reads the next until the passage is completed. This keeps everyone involved. After reading these passages, I intend that they be seriously considered as they relate to the primary Scripture at hand in Hebrews. At times, this relationship seems to be available and obvious on the surface. In many other instances, the interconnectedness of the whole of Scripture and its principles are most effectively understood through deeper thought, discussion, and prayer along the way.

In commenting on and discussing the various Scriptures, questions, concepts and principles in this material, it is not required that any particular person give their input. The reader of any passage may, but is not required to, give their thoughts to the group. This is a group participation exercise for the mutual benefit of all involved and many people in the group giving their insight into a certain passage or question will often enhance the learning experience.

I also have two practical suggestions if you do this in a small group setting. Every time you meet, I suggest you review the calendar and go over meetings scheduled for the future and who will be bringing refreshments. This makes things run a lot better while enhancing everyone's enjoyment and expectations.

Background to the Book of Hebrews

WARREN W. WIERSBE tells a story about a man from Leeds, England, who visited his audiologist to have his failing hearing evaluated. The man had already been wearing a hearing aid for over twenty years. In order to perform the test, the man needed to remove his hearing aid. His hearing immediately improved. This was not, as you might imagine, a miraculous spiritual healing. The man had simply been wearing the hearing aid in the wrong ear for most of his adult life.

This story dramatizes the problems that most non-Jewish believers have had in understanding the book of Hebrews over the centuries. The early Jewish believers had no trouble whatsoever understanding what this book was telling them. With their foundation in the Tanakh (the Old Testament), the illustrations, explanations, and teaching were all quite clear to them. However, since at this point in time most believers are not Jewish and do not have a strong foundation in the Old Testament, they have a very difficult time with this book of the Bible as a whole. In fact, the solution to this dilemma adopted by many denominations and seminary professors has been to either ignore it or incorrectly allegorize things so that they are understandable to their scholastically challenged and admittedly Gentile understanding of this material.

We, however, do not want to be guilty of this error. It is our goal to understand what God is telling us in this important portion of Scripture as fully as possible.

To that end, we must continue to educate ourselves about the foundations of the book that lie in the Tanakh. This will enable us to better understand just what the author was saying then, while also helping us to more accurately apply it to our lives today.

This concept may sound strange to some, but it is not. The Judeo-Christian Scriptures are a fully integrated message system. Every word, every form of punctuation, every place name, is there by design. To fully appreciate the riches that await the reader, one must diligently avail oneself of the fullness of the documents themselves to see how they work together in a supernatural fashion to communicate God's message to us.

Remarkably, the documents that make up the Judeo-Christian Scriptures were written over thousands of years, yet they validate one another from beginning to end. Any apparent contradictions disappear upon diligent study. This is even more amazing when we realize this group of writings was set down over thousands of years by at least forty different people. For the most part, they had no communication with one another, and yet what they wrote is unbelievably consistent. Add to that the fact that history, science, archaeology, linguistics, and experience all validate this book that we call the Bible, and it becomes all the more amazing.

There is, perhaps, one unnecessary page in most Bibles printed today. That is the blank page separating the Old and New Testaments. It all works together and flows together in perfect harmony if one will take the time to understand it without interjecting personal presuppositions.

So who wrote this book? The answer, hotly debated over the years, is actually quite simple.

First of all, it had to be someone who understood the Old Testament prophecies and their fulfillment in Jesus Christ. Revelation 19:10 says, "For the essence of prophecy is to give a clear witness for Jesus" (NLT). This person was inspired by God and wrote a book entirely consistent with the rest of the New and Old Testament.

Some scholars have hotly debated just which human being God used for this purpose. While this actually has no bearing on the veracity of the Scriptures or the sustenance we find therein, it is somewhat interesting.

Many people believe the letter was written by Paul for several reasons. This list is not exhaustive, and one cannot claim with absolute certainty that the conclusion is correct. However, I believe that a good lawyer with this evidence at their fingertips could prove the case for Paul's authorship in a court of law.

Some reasons in favor of Paul's authorship of Hebrews:

1. As we said, it was written by someone with an exhaustive knowledge of the Old Testament documents. Paul was one of the most intelligent and most highly educated men of his day, having sat under the teaching of Gamaliel, the most famous of the Jewish teachers of the time.

2. Peter seems to indicate that it was written by Paul in 2 Peter 3:15-16. Here Peter seems to reference a letter written by Paul to the Hebrews. All of Paul's other letters were written to Gentile believers. Peter also says that Paul has written about some things that are difficult to understand, which the author of Hebrews has indeed done, particularly in Hebrews 6 and 10.

3. Hebrews 10:30 refers to Deuteronomy 32:35-36. The quote from Deuteronomy 32:36 is an exact quote from the Hebrew and the one from Deuteronomy 32:35 is a paraphrase. This is interesting since the same paraphrase appears in Romans 12:19, which was indisputably written by Paul. It would appear, then, that Paul was fond of paraphrasing Deuteronomy 32:35 in this fashion. Certainly others could have copied him, but the circumstantial evidence for the same use of this paraphrase in two places seems to point to Paul.

4. In 2 Thessalonians 3:17-18, Paul signs his letter by saying "The grace of our Lord Jesus Christ be with you all. Amen." This same reference to grace appears in a number of his other letters, most notably in Romans 16:24, 1 Corinthians 16:23-24, 2 Corinthians 13:14, Galatians 6:18, Ephesians 6:24, Philippians 4:23, Colossians 4:18, 1 Thessalonians 5:28, 2 Thessalonians 3:18, 1 Timothy 6:21, 2 Timothy 4:22, Titus 3:15, and Philemon 25. So why is this such a big deal? First of all, Hebrews 13:25 has the same reference. And it is important to note that the word "grace"

does not appear anywhere else in the other epistles, except for 2 Peter 3:18, where it is used differently. (Peter uses it as an exhortation or instruction, and not as a salutation or blessing as Paul does in his letters.)

5. Romans 8:35-39 lists 17 things that can separate one from the love of Christ. In Hebrews 12:18-24 and Galatians 5:19-21 we find that Paul has used lists in a similar fashion to explain things to his readers. Linguistic experts who have studied style are taken by the similarities of these passages, according to Dr. Chuck Missler, in his commentary on James.

6. In Habakkuk 2:4, we see that "The just shall live by faith." The book of Romans defines which people constitute the just. The book of Galatians defines how they shall live. The book of Hebrews seems to complete this Old Testament exposition as it speaks of faith. Again, it seems as though the same person wrote all three books.

7. Hebrews 10:15 and Romans 8:16 seem to be similar statements of the same concept. The same is true of 1 Corinthians 3:13 and Hebrews 5:12-14. This in and of itself is not proof since Scripture always validates itself. However, it may point to Paul's authorship.

8. In Hebrews 13:18, the writer says "Pray for us." The only other epistle writer who makes this request is Paul.

9. In Hebrews 13, we see that Timothy accompanies the writer of Hebrews. We know that Timothy accompanied Paul from 2 Corinthians 1:1, Colossians 1:1, and 1 Thessalonians 1:1. While this does not mean that Timothy did not travel with anyone else, we have no evidence of him doing so.

So if Paul did write Hebrews, why didn't he just say so?

Perhaps this is because he was primarily the apostle to the Gentiles (Acts 9:15). In our study of Romans we saw how much Paul wanted to see the Jewish people come to know their own Messiah, Yeshua Ha-Mashiach. And yet those with a background in Judaism initially opposed him (Acts 21:27-28 and Acts 22:17-22).

Interestingly, if Paul did write Hebrews and purposely did not sign it to make it more palatable and available to those Jews who initially opposed him, we are also provided with a possible answer to those who say that the linguistic style of Hebrews in the original language is somewhat different than that of Paul's letters that he did sign. If he was purposely concealing his authorship, Paul might have indeed employed a somewhat different style. It is also possible that he simply dictated the book to a different person with a different educational background from his amanuensis in his other letters.

Assuming we are correct that Paul did write Hebrews, he was faced with the task of utilizing exclusively Jewish arguments from the Tanakh (Old Testament) to exalt Jesus Christ, without antagonizing his readers who might be prejudiced against him because of his association with the Gentiles. What better way to do this than to use his knowledge of Judaism and the Scriptures to construct a helpful letter and to send it anonymously.

We know that in many ways the Old Testament is the New Testament concealed, and the New Testament is the Old Testament revealed. This is exactly what we see going on here. The book of Hebrews is in many ways like a New Testament Leviticus, in which the things alluded to in that book from the Tanakh are explained.

As we go through this book we will notice eight major themes. They include:

1. The idea that Jews must leave the shadows of a relationship with God behind and exchange them for the real thing.

2. The concept that the ceremonies and traditions that make up Judaism were a precursor to things to come. Those things have now come and should be enjoyed by the Jews instead of the "shadows" of the real things.

3. There were many models or "types" in the Old Testament that have now been fulfilled by the Jewish Messiah in the New Testament.

4. The reader is constantly encouraged to exchange the good things of Judaism for the better things that have now come. It in no way diminishes the past, but helps the reader see the fulfillment of the Tanakh in Jesus Christ.

5. The author continually examines the inadequacy of the law and the perfect nature of the new covenant.

6. The Old Testament ordinances with a temporary purpose are explained, and their replacement with eternal realities is examined.

7. The conditional promises of the past are contrasted with the unconditional promises available through the person of the Yeshua Ha-Mashiach, Jesus Christ, the Jewish Messiah.

8. Finally, and of vital importance, we constantly see that the Old and New Testament concepts of trust and obedience go hand in hand. This message cannot be ignored and works perfectly in combination with the overriding messages from the books of James and Romans. To many, Romans seems to accentuate the grace of God. At the same time, James accentuates the fact that one's faith must be accompanied by a life well-lived in obedience to the Word of God. Hebrews puts it together. Trust and obedience are, and must be, two sides of the same coin in the life of the believer.

And that, my friends, is more of an introduction than I intended, and certainly more than is needed to enjoy this special book which we are now privileged to study.

WEEK 1

SUPERIOR TO THE ANGELS
HEBREWS 1:1-14

Opening Prayer

Group Warm-Up Question

How do you think you might react if you saw an angel?

Read Hebrews 1:1-14

Read Hebrews 1:1 again.

How did God communicate to people in the past?

In what ways were the prophets different from Jesus Christ?

Read and comment on the following verses regarding this:

Isaiah 6:5

Daniel 10:7-8

Psalm 51:9-10

1 Peter 1:10

Read Hebrews 1:2 again.
How has God spoken to us during "these last days?"

What special activities and honors has God accorded to Jesus?

How does the concept of the Son being heir to all things relate to us?

Read and comment on the following verses:

Galatians 4:1-7

Romans 8:14-17

Exactly what does it mean when Hebrews 1:2 says that everything was made through the Son?

Read the following verses and expand on this idea:

John 1:3

Colossians 1:16-17

Read Hebrews 1:3 again.

This verse is packed with more information than one can take in on a single pass.

What does it mean when it says that Christ is the express image of God's being?

Read and comment on the following verses:

    1 Timothy 6:15-16

    Colossians 1:15

What does Hebrews 1:3 mean when it says that all things are upheld by the power of His word?

Read Genesis 1:2.

The word used for "upholding" in Hebrews 1:3 is exactly the same word used for "moving" in the Septuagint, the Greek translation of the Old Testament.

Read Colossians 1:16-17 and comment.

What does it mean to you in your daily life when you realize the fullness of power spoken of in these verses?

What does it mean in Hebrews 1:3 when it says that "He had by Himself purged our sins" (KJV)?

It is important for us to realize that the Greek tense of the verb "purged" in this statement indicates this action "is completed, it is done, it is finished." There is no room for ambiguity here. This verse also says that Jesus sat down on the right hand of God. We should realize that sitting implies several things.

Read the following verses to understand what is implied here:

> Job 29:7-8
>
> Daniel 7:9-10
>
> Revelation 5:13
>
> Exodus 15:6
>
> Hebrews 10:11-12

Read Hebrews 1:4-14 again.

To get a better idea of what the statements in this passage mean when they refer to angels, we need to understand this from the perspective of a Jewish background. To help us understand that the Old Testament writers regarded angels as the most exalted of God's created creatures, read the following verses and list what we learn about angels.

> Acts 7:52-53
>
> Deuteronomy 33:2 (in the King James Version)
>
>> Note: Here we see God coming with 10,000 "saints." The actual term is the same one used in Psalm 68:17 for angels.
>
> Galatians 3:19
>
> Matthew 16:27

Psalm 103:20

Psalm 104:4

Daniel 7:10

Revelation 5:11

2 Kings 6:15-17

We also see angels interacting with and for believers in the following verses:

Daniel 6:22

Acts 5:17-19

Acts 12:6-9

Read: Hebrews 1:4-14 again.

Compare and contrast the position of Jesus Christ and that of angels.

Position of Christ	Position of the Angels
1.	1.
2.	2.
3.	3.
4.	4.
5.	5.

It is also important to realize that these verses in Hebrews correlate perfectly with the Old Testament.

Read the following verses together:

> Hebrews 1:5 and Psalm 2:6-7
>
> Hebrews 1:6 and Psalm 97:7
>
>> Note: This is even clearer in the Septuagint which translates more precisely to "Worship Him, all ye angels."
>
> Hebrews 1:7 and Psalm 104:4
>
> Hebrews 1:8 and Isaiah 9:6-7
>
> Hebrews 1:10 and Psalm 102:25
>
> Hebrews 1:11-12 and Psalm 102:25-27
>
> Hebrews 1:13 and Psalm 110:1
>
> Hebrews 1:9 and Psalm 45:6-7

Read: Psalm 45:6-7 again.

There appear to be two contrasting and important sides to Christ's reign. What are they?

How does this relate to the following verses?

> John 14:21
>
> Amos 5:5-6

Revelation 2:6

Jude 4

1 John 5:3-5

1 Thessalonians 5:21-22

How should this concept and the inherent commands then impact the way we live?

Read Hebrews 1:14 again and comment on it in relation to:

1 Thessalonians 5:9

1 Peter 1:3-4

Application Question

After thinking more about Christ and the angels, we find a paradox: Jesus Christ is superior to the angels and, at the same time, entered the world as a man (lower than the angels).

1. How would you explain this to someone?

2. What does it mean to you on a personal basis in your day to day life?

Close in prayer.

Review calendar.

Assign refreshments for next time.

WEEK 2

LISTEN UP!
HEBREWS 2:1-4

Opening Prayer

Group Warm-Up Question

What trouble have you gotten into by not heeding a warning, following instructions, or paying attention? Think of at least one example.

Read Hebrews 2:1-4

What did the writer of Hebrews want his readers to pay attention to?

Why is this so vitally important?

What happens when a person does not follow this admonition?

Read Hebrews 12:14-29 and enumerate some of the things that happen when one neglects the Word of God:

1.

2.

3.

4.

5.

6.

Is it too strong a statement to say that neglecting the Word of God leads to defying it?

The ancient Israelites felt that anyone who neglected the law was excluded from the world to come. Some teachers taught that this sin was unpardonable. In Judaism, deliberate acts had greater negative consequences than those that were "accidental."

Do these ancient traditions and thoughts from Judaism have any relevance to our world and lives today?

Read Luke 12:48.

Why do you think that God is stricter with those who have received more revelation than others?

At one time I heard Paul Anderson, "The World's Strongest Man," say that this was his favorite verse. Why might that have been?

Read Deuteronomy 18:19.

How seriously does God regard not listening to his message?

Read Deuteronomy 18:20.

How seriously does God regard anyone who distorts his message?

Read Hebrews 2:2 again.

What happened to people in the past when they neglected or purposely violated God's law?

What is the consequence for people today who purposefully pay no attention to the great gift offered by Jesus Christ himself?

Read Hebrews 2:3 again.

Who specifically passed on the good news spoken of by Jesus Christ?

What characteristics did these people have in common?

Read Hebrews 2:4 again.

How did God validate the message delivered by Jesus Christ?

Read and comment on the following verses:

 Isaiah 46:10

 Mark 16:17-20

 Acts 2:43

To better understand the fabulous import of one of the ways the Creator of the Universe has validated His Word and the work and person of Jesus Christ, it is helpful to get a grasp on composite probability theory and its application to the Judeo-Christian Scriptures.

We are indebted to Peter W. Stoner, past chairman of the Department of Mathematics and Astronomy at Pasadena City College as well as to Dr. Robert C. Newman with his Ph.D. in astrophysics from Cornell University for the initial statistical work on this topic. Their joint efforts on composite probability theory were first published in the book *Science Speaks.*

Composite Probability Theory

If something has a 1 in 10 chance of occurring, that is easy for us to understand. It means that 10 percent of the time, the event will happen. However, when we calculate the probability of several different events occurring at the same time, the odds of that happening decrease exponentially. This is the basic premise behind composite probability theory.

If two events have a 1 in 10 chance of happening, the chance that both of these will occur is 1 in 10 x 10, or 1 in 100. To show this numerically, this probability would be 1 in 10^2, with the 1 in superscript indicating how many tens are being multiplied. If we have 10^3, it means that we have a number of 1,000. Thus, 10^4 is equivalent to 10,000, and so on. This is referred to as 10 to the first power, 10 to the second power, 10 to the third power, and so on.

For example, let's assume that there are ten people in a room. If one of the ten is left handed and one of the ten has red hair; the probability that any one person in the room will be left handed and have red hair is one in one hundred.

We can apply this model to the prophecy revealed in the Bible to figure out the mathematical chances of Jesus' birth, life, and death, in addition to many other events occurring in the New Testament by chance. To demonstrate this, we will consider eight prophecies about Jesus and assign a probability of them occurring individually by chance. To eliminate any disagreement, we will be more limiting than necessary. Furthermore, we will use the prophecies that are arguably the most unlikely to be fulfilled by chance. I think you will agree that in doing so, we are severely handicapping ourselves.

The first prophecy from Micah 5:2 says: "But you, O Bethlehem Ephrathah, are only a small village in Judah. Yet a ruler of Israel will come from you, one whose origins are from the distant past" (NLT). This prophecy tells us that the Messiah will be born in Bethlehem. What is the chance of that actually occurring? As we consider this, we also have to ask: What is the probability that anyone in the history of the world might be born in this obscure town? When we take into account all the people who ever lived, this might conservatively be 1 in 200,000.

Let's move on to the second prophecy in Zechariah 9:9: "Rejoice greatly, O people of Zion! Shout in triumph, O people of Jerusalem! Look, your king is coming to you. He is righteous and victorious, yet he is humble, riding on a donkey—even on a donkey's colt" (NLT). For our purposes, we can assume that the chance that the Messiah (the king) riding into Jerusalem on a donkey might be 1 in 100. But, really, how many kings in the history of the world have actually done this?

The third prophecy is from Zechariah 11:12: "I said to them, 'If you like, give me my wages, whatever I am worth; but only if you want to.' So they counted out for my wages thirty pieces of silver" (NLT). What is the chance that someone would be betrayed and that the price of that betrayal would be thirty pieces of silver? For our purposes, let's assume the chance that anyone in the history of the world would be betrayed for thirty pieces of silver might be 1 in 1,000.

The fourth prophecy comes from Zechariah 11:13: "And the Lord said to me, 'Throw it to the potter'—this magnificent sum at which they valued me! So I took the thirty coins and threw them to the potter in the Temple of the Lord" (NLT). Now we need to consider what the chances would be that a temple and a potter would be involved in someone's betrayal. For our statistical model, let's assume this is 1 in 100,000.

The fifth prophecy in Zechariah 13:6 reads: "And one shall say unto him, What are these wounds in thine hands? Then he shall answer, Those with which I was wounded in the house of my friends" (KJV). The question here is, "How many people in the history of the world have died with wounds in their hands?" I believe we can safely assume that the chance of any person dying with wounds in his or her hands is somewhat greater than 1 in 1,000.

The sixth prophecy in Isaiah 53:7 states, "He was oppressed and treated harshly, yet he never said a word. He was led like a lamb to the slaughter. And as a sheep is silent before the shearers, he did not open his mouth" (NLT). This raises a particularly tough question. How many people in the history of the world can we imagine being put on trial, knowing that they were innocent, without making one statement in their defense? For our statistical model, let's say this is 1 in 1,000, although it is pretty hard to imagine.

Moving on to the seventh prophecy, Isaiah 53:9 says, "He had done no wrong and had never deceived anyone. But he was buried like a criminal; he was put in a rich man's grave" (NLT). Here we need to consider how many people, out of all the good individuals in the world who have died, have died a criminal's death and been buried in a rich person's grave? These people died out of place. (Some might also infer that they were buried out of place, though that is not necessarily true.) Let's assume that the chance of a good person dying as a criminal and being buried with the rich is about 1 in 1,000.

The eighth and final prophecy is from Psalm 22:16: "My enemies surround me like a pack of dogs; an evil gang closes in on me. They have pierced my hands and feet" (NLT). Remember that this passage and all the other prophetic references to the crucifixion were written before this form of execution was even invented.

However, for our purposes, we just need to consider the probability of someone in the history of the world being executed in this way. Certainly, Jesus wasn't the only person killed by crucifixion. We will say that the chances of a person dying from this specific form of execution to be at 1 in 10,000.

CALCULATING THE RESULTS

To determine the chance that all these things would happen to the same person by chance, we simply multiply the fraction of each of the eight probabilities. When we do, we get a chance of 1 in 10^{28}. In other words, the probability is 1 in 10,000,000,000,000,000,000,000,000,000. Would you bet against these odds?

Unfortunately, there is another blow coming for those who do not believe that the Bible is true or that Jesus is who He said He was. There are not just eight prophecies of this nature in the Bible that were fulfilled in Jesus Christ—there are *more than three hundred* such prophecies in the Old Testament. The prophecies we looked at were just the ones that we could *most easily* show fulfilled.

If we deal with only forty-eight prophecies about Jesus, based on the above numbers, the chance that Jesus is not who He said He was or that the Bible is not true is 1 in 10^{168}. This is a larger number than most of us can grasp (though you may want to try to write it sometime). To give you some perspective on just how big this number is, consider these statistics from the book "Science Speaks" by Peter Stoner:

- If the state of Texas were buried in silver dollars two feet deep, it would be covered by 10^{17} silver dollars.
- In the history of the world, only 10^{11} people have supposedly ever lived. (I don't know who counted this.)
- There are 10^{17} seconds in 1 billion years.
- Scientists tell us that there are 10^{66} atoms in the universe and 10^{80} particles in the universe.

- Looking at just forty-eight prophecies out of more than three hundred, there is only a 1 in 10^{168} chance of Jesus not being who He said He was or the Bible being wrong.

In probability theory, the threshold for an occurrence being absurd—translate that as "impossible"—is only 10^{50}. No thinking person who understands these simple probabilities can deny the reality of our faith or the Bible based on intellect. Every person who has set out to disprove the Judeo-Christian Scriptures on an empirical basis has ended up proving the Bible's authenticity and has, in most cases, become a believer.

These facts are more certain than any others in the world. However, not everyone who has come to realize the reliability and reality of these documents has become a believer. These intelligent people who understand the statistical impossibility that Jesus was not who He claimed to be and who yet do not make a decision for Christ are not insane; they generally just have embedded emotional issues. They allow these issues to stop them from enjoying the many experiential benefits that God offers through His Word and the dynamic relationship they could have with Him, not to mention longer-term benefits. These people, of course, deserve love and prayer, because this is not just a matter of the intellect. If it were, every intelligent inquirer would be a believer. Rather, it is very much a matter of the heart, the emotions, and the spirit.

The truth of this statement was brought home to me in one very poignant situation. In this case, someone very near and dear to me said "But dad, this could have been anybody." No, this could not have been just anybody. The chance that these prophecies could have been fulfilled in one person is so remote as to be absurd. That is impossible. Only one person in human history fulfilled these prophecies and that person is Jesus Christ. To claim otherwise is not intelligent, it is not smart, it is not well-considered, and it is not honest. It may be emotionally satisfying, but in all other respects it is self-delusional.

Read Ephesians 1:9-11.

When did God come up with this plan?

Read the following verses:

>   Romans 8:28

>   Romans 12:2

What special privileges in life do believers have as a result of this plan?

Read Romans 8:16 and comment.

In addition to His Word, how else does God communicate with us?

Read 1 John 5:1-13 and tie all of the concepts we have been discussing together as we go through it verse by verse.

Application Question

What can you do to be sure that you personally pay close attention to God's Word on a daily, hourly and minute by minute basis?

Close in prayer.

Review calendar.

Assign refreshments for next time.

WEEK 3

REAL FREEDOM
HEBREWS 2:5-18

Opening Prayer

Group Warm-Up Question

What does it mean to you to be free?

Read Hebrews 2:5-18

Read Hebrews 2:5-8 again.

What place is being referred to in these verses?

The Greek word used for "the world to come" or "the future world" in Hebrews 2:5 is *oikuomene* which means "the habitable place." This word is used 15 times in the New Testament and in 13 of those times it is used to refer to the earth.

19

Read Matthew 19:28-30, which shows us that this is the millenial kingdom.

To learn more about what is alluded to in these four verses, read:

> Genesis 1:26-27
>
> Psalm 8:4-6
>
> Romans 8:17
>
> Revelation 21:7

Note: In God's Word we read about four specific phases of the earth. They are:
1. The time before Adam
2. The present
3. The millenial kingdom on this earth
4. The new earth

Read Hebrews 2:8 again.

What is the relationship between Jesus Christ and the rest of the universe?

Read Hebrews 2:9 again.

What did Christ do that led to his current exalted status at the right hand of the throne of God?

What was unique about the death that Christ suffered?

Did He anticipate his death with a certainty and purpose beyond any other death in human history?

Read and comment on the following verses:

> Matthew 16:21
>
> John 2:4
>
> John 3:16 (Jesus speaking.)

Read Hebrews 2:10 again.

What is God's ultimate plan for believers?

Read and discuss the following verses:

> John 17:22-24
>
> Colossians 3:4

What does it mean that God made Jesus a "perfect leader?"

The Greek word for leader in Hebrews 2:10 is *archegos*, and means captain, pioneer, leader, or champion. The term was used for both human and divine heroes, founders of schools, or those who cut a path forward for their followers and whose exploits for humanity were rewarded by exaltation. In addition, we should note that when it says that Jesus became our perfect leader, it does not imply that he was previously imperfect. The word translated as "perfect" means "complete, effective, and adequate" in the Greek.

How does our understanding of the Greek influence our understanding of this description of Jesus as our "perfect leader?"

Read 1 Corinthians 8:6 and discuss what else we learn about our perfect leader. (Read in the New Living Translation or the King James Version.)

Read Hebrews 2:11-12 again.

What *does* Christ do to qualify a person for membership in the family of God?

What *did* Christ do to qualify a person to become a member of God's family?

Read and explain the following verses:

     John 17:17-19

     Psalm 22:1-22

Psalm 22:1-22 is one of the most amazing passages in the Old Testament. When one realizes that it talks about Jesus Christ hundreds of years before his death and resurrection, it becomes even more meaningful. In considering this, we should remember what we learned about Composite Probability Theory in Lesson 2 entitled "Listen Up."

To help bring this home, please list all of the allusions to Jesus Christ that you find in this passage.

1.

2.

3.

4.

5.

6.

7.

8.

9.

10.

Read and tie together:

Hebrews 2:13

Isaiah 8:17-18

The Old Testament also goes on to speak of Christ in another interesting fashion in:

Isaiah 8:14-15

Isaiah 28:16

Psalm 118:22

This is further confirmed in the New Testament in:

>Romans 9:32-33

>1 Peter 2:6-8

Read Hebrews 2:14-15 again.

What effect did the death of Christ have upon the power of Satan?

The Greek word that is here translated "destroy" in most versions of the Bible, including the KJV, NIV and the GNT, does not mean to annihilate. Satan is obviously still at work in the world. The Greek word means "render inoperative, make of none effect." Satan is not annihilated, but he is disarmed in terms of death and can be defeated in the life of a believer.

Why are human beings so naturally afraid of dying?

Do believers need to have this fear? Why or why not?

Read Hebrews 2:16-17 again.

Why was it necessary for Jesus to be like us?

Here we also see it stated, and apparently accepted by all without dispute, that God sent Jesus to the Jews (the descendants of Abraham). However, we also see in Romans 11:1-31 that when some Jews rejected their Messiah, this resulted in the good news also being available to Gentiles.

Read Hebrews 2:18, and then read it again in the King James Version.

Why is this verse and concept so vitally important for a believer to live a victorious life?

In the Greek, the word used for "succor" in the King James Version, or "help" in more modern language, literally means "to run to the cry of a child; to bring help when it is needed." What further insights does this understanding of the Greek give us?

Application Question

What advice would you give to a friend who has trusted Jesus Christ with their life and still harbors a fear of death?

Close in prayer.

Review calendar.

Assign refreshments for next time.

WEEK 4

JESUS AND MOSES
HEBREWS 3:1-6

Opening Prayer

Group Warm-Up Question

Who are (or were) some of the people you regard as heroes?

Read Hebrews 3:1-6

Read Hebrews 3:1 again.

How does the author of Hebrews address those to whom the letter is written?

What does this tell us about their position in relationship to Jesus Christ?

Why is this important to realize?

What important command do we also find in Hebrews 3:1?

Read the following verses:

> Hebrews 12:3
>
> Colossians 3:16
>
> 2 Timothy 1:14
>
> 2 Corinthians 6:16
>
> 2 Corinthians 12:9
>
> Ephesians 3:17
>
> Ephesians 2:22
>
> James 4:5
>
> 1 Corinthians 3:16

What else does thinking or dwelling upon Jesus imply or bring about?

Depending upon the version you are reading, you will find that in Hebrews 3:1 Jesus Christ is referred to as a messenger, a prophet, or an apostle. Conversely, he is referred to as a high priest in the same sentence. It is important for us to realize what these two very different terms mean.

A prophet, messenger, or an apostle is God's representative to people. This term means "one sent with a commission." Such a person may foretell, exhort, and speak God's Word as they present God to men and women.

A high priest represents men and women before God. He presents people to God.

What important truths from the Scriptures do we have reiterated to us as we realize that both of these terms apply simultaneously to Jesus Christ?

Read Hebrews 3:3-6 again, paying careful attention to how Moses and Jesus are both similar and different. We should pay attention to the metaphor of houses in doing this, and count how many times the word *house* or *household* is used in these verses, and how it is used.

Among them you will find:

The House of Israel

The Household or Family of God

The House of God (As the Holy Spirit indwells a person.)

Contrasting and Comparing Jesus and Moses in Hebrews 3:3-6, we find seven ways in which Jesus is similar to and yet superior to Moses. Check them off below as you find them in Hebrews 3:3-6.

Moses	Jesus
Messenger or apostle	The Messenger
Just a man	Fully God
Member of a house	Built the house
Involved in a single house	Built all houses
Servant of God	Son of God
Spoke of Truths to be Revealed	Fulfillment
Servant in His house	Son over the house

Why is Jesus worthy of more honor than Moses?

Read Hebrews 3:6 again.

How does biblical hope differ from the ordinary hope spoken of in society today?

Biblical hope is defined as confidence, sureness, and knowledge of future things; certainty that is stronger than knowing; an ultimate, internal, overpowering, all-enveloping, eternal surety and absolute truth.

Read II Timothy 2:12 and further discuss the concept of Biblical hope.

How is our membership in God's household demonstrated?

Hebrews 3:6 speaks of keeping up our courage and remaining confident in our hope. This is not a conditional statement, but a statement of evidence. That is, if we exhibit these things, they are evidence we belong to God through Jesus Christ.

Relate this to the following verses:

Colossians 1:21-23

Colossians 1:3-6

Colossians 1:27

Colossians 1:10

1 Peter 1:13

Titus 2:11-14

Why is keeping up our courage as well as remaining confident in our hope such a powerful concept? This seems to be going beyond the already powerful concept of biblical hope.

How should our identity as believers and members of God's household impact the way we live our lives each day?

Application Question

What Scriptural promise or concept can you hold on to this week to help you live the victorious life to which you are called as a follower of Jesus Christ?

Close in prayer.

Review calendar.

Assign refreshments for next week.

WEEK 5

DIRE WARNING AGAINST UNBELIEF
HEBREWS 3:7-19

Opening Prayer

Group Warm-Up Question

Why do you think some people follow Christ for a short while and then seem to drop out or turn away? (1 John 2:19 may be of interest as we consider this question.)

Read Hebrews 3:7-19

In order to understand what the writer of Hebrews referred to, we must look back to the Old Testament.

Read Psalm 95:7-11.

Read Hebrews 3:7 again.

To whom does the author of Hebrews ascribe Psalm 95:7-11?

Why is this important?

To see the involvement of what we call the Trinity in Scripture, read the following verses:

Hebrews 1:1

Hebrews 2:3

Hebrews 3:7

Read Hebrews 3:8-10 again.

Why was God angry with the Israelites who escaped their enslavement in Egypt?

How did these particular Israelites try God's patience?

What does it mean that their hearts turned away from God and that they refused to do what God told them?

To understand this, we must again return to the Old Testament. Here we find some of the things that God wanted the Israelites to do that they turned away from.

Read and explain the following verses:

Psalm 68:4

Psalm 145:17

Psalm 143:5

Psalm 119:27

Psalm 119:32

Psalm 119:33

Psalm 119:35

Read Deuteronomy 9:24 to see what Moses had to say about this situation.

How was God's rescue of the Israelites from their slavery in Egypt similar to what He has done for us today?

God uses several motifs time and again in His Word, and it appears that we can recognize one of them here.

Read Colossians 1:13-14 and explain.

To understand what happened to the Israelites after they escaped from Egypt, read Numbers 13 and 14. As we read this very interesting, instructive, and long passage, we should be on the lookout for continued use of motifs that might be instructive to us.

Many people might wonder why God would eventually drive out the inhabitants established in this land that God had promised to the Jews. Besides His promise to the Jews, we find important information in Deuteronomy 9:4.

What principles of corporate and national responsibility do we find in this verse? (These principles are repeated time and again in Scripture.)

What implications does this have for us today?

Read again:

Numbers 14:40

Hebrews 3:7

Hebrews 3:13

Hebrews 3:15

What implications does this have for our obedience to God in our lives right now?

Does this mean that if we don't follow God's instructions today, that we might not get another chance? Might we not ever get another chance?

What might the experience of the Jews and their wilderness wanderings in the desert represent to believers during the times in which we live? Remember the use of patterns and motif in Scripture as we consider this question.

Some say that the wanderings of the Jews in the desert for 40 years signifies believers today who fail to claim their spiritual inheritance in Christ and waste their lives, sometimes even doubting God's Word and living in restless unbelief. Do you agree or disagree with this comparison?

To what might the inheritance spoken of in Numbers represent to believers today? Read the following verses and explain.

Ephesians 1:3

Ephesians 1:11

Ephesians 1:15-23

Read Hebrews 3:11-14.

In reading Numbers 13 and 14, we see that while the actions of the Israelites resulted in them losing the rewards in Canaan, God did not reject them. How does this relate to believers whose actions limit the blessing they receive from God today?

Read Hebrews 3:12 again.

The Greek word used for "turning away from the living God" is used in Hebrews only once, and that is right here. This is where we get the English word *apostasy*. From the context and the comparison with the Israelites and their experience in Egypt we see that this refers to the Israelites or people now stubbornly going their own way and subsequently being disciplined by God. Again, we see the possibility of missing out on the inheritance of God's blessings in one's life today.

What is the import of someone turning away from "the Living God?"

Does this make you uncomfortable? It should.

Read the following verses and explain:

Matthew 16:16

1 Timothy 4:10

2 Corinthians 6:16

1 Corinthians 3:16

Read Hebrews 3:13 again.

What do we learn about the deceitfulness of sin spoken of in this verse?

Read the following verses for more insight into the deceitfulness of sin and explain what they mean:

Ephesians 4:21-22

Matthew 13:22

2 Thessalonians 2:9-10

Colossians 2:8

2 Peter 2:13

The fact that sin is difficult for humans to handle, as we see in the above verses, or that we are forgiven and secure, as we see in John 10:28-29 and Romans 8:9, is not a license to sin, as we see in Romans 6:1-2.

What command do we also find in Hebrews 3:13?

Why is this command so important? (This command also infers that we have a choice.)

Read the following verses and explain and expand upon this:

Matthew 13:20-21

Acts 11:22-23

Acts 13:43

Acts 14:21-22

Philippians 2:12

1 Peter 1:5

Read Hebrews 3:15-19.

How do we "hear God's voice" in our lives today?

Read 2 Timothy 3:16-17 again and memorize it.

What does it mean to "harden one's heart?"

Here we see the use of the word *sklerotes* in the Greek, which means a gradual, continual, stubborn, and obstinate hardening of the heart and will. This is the root of the English word "arteriosclerosis," which refers to a gradual and continuing hardening of the physical heart and arteries.

In verse 15, the term used for "heart" means the "seat of the will" in Greek. This is an issue of choice.

There are consequences for not trusting God, as we see by reading:

> Exodus 17:1-7
>
> Numbers 20:7-12
>
> 1 Corinthians 10:1-5

Archaeologist Bob Cornuke has identified what he believes to be this rock in the Sinai desert. There actually still exists a very large rock that bears the marks of water flowing out of it in times past. It has been preserved in this arid climate and is generally now inaccessible, as are many other Biblical archaeological treasures now within the borders of modern day Saudi Arabia.

We then see this rock motif continued in the following verses:

Deuteronomy 30:15

2 Samuel 22:2

Psalm 95:1

Isaiah 32:2

Matthew 16:15-18 (The rock is Jesus Christ, not Peter.)

Matthew 21:42

Read John 4:1-15 and discuss how this relates to the concept of the rock and the Water of Life in the Old and New Testaments.

Read Hebrews 3:18-19 again.

The same Greek word translated here in the context of the rest of the passage as "unbelief" is translated as "obey not" in two important places in Romans. The concepts of believing and obeying are built out of the same Greek word. To see this, read Romans 2:8 and Romans 10:21.

Unbelief implies a refusal to heed God's Word. This is actually evidencing contempt for God's Word, a very serious thing. Unbelief is an act of the heart, an act of the will, and an overt refusal to listen to God as He communicates to us through His Word.

Is it also possible for unbelief to be the result of neglect of God's Word?

How does understanding the way unbelief and disobedience work together impact your understanding?

Is there a prerequisite for receiving the unconditional promises of God? Must one claim them?

Conversely, how do belief (as it relates to heeding the Word of God) and obedience work together in the day to day life of a believer? (See the old hymn "Trust and Obey" at the end of this material.)

Internationally known Bible Scholar Chuck Missler says that the Old Testament concept of obedience is the equivalent of the New Testament concept of believing. They work together.

Discuss how this concept relates to the following verses.

> Philippians 2:5-18
>
> Revelation 3:14-22
>
> 1 John 5:4-5
>
> John 14:6

What are the consequences when believers fail to encourage each other and hold each other accountable?

Application Question

What routine can you set up this next month to be sure that your heart is correctly inclined toward God?

We must continue to abide in Jesus Christ. We are rescued by God's grace and must remain rooted in His Word as we act in the world.

How Composer John H. Sammis Wrote the Hymn "Trust and Obey"

John H. Sammis (1846-1919) gave up his life as a businessman and part-time YMCA worker to study for the ministry. He was ordained a Presbyterian minister in 1880 and then served at several pastorates. In his later years, Sammis taught at the Bible Institute of Los Angeles.

Daniel B. Towner (1850-1919) was music director for several well-known churches and schools, including the Moody Bible Institute. He published several music books and wrote the music for many well-loved hymns, including "At Calvary" and "Only A Sinner Saved By Grace."

In 1887, just following an evangelistic meeting held by Dwight L. Moody, a young man stood to share his story in an after-service testimony meeting. As he was speaking, it became clear to many that he knew little about the Bible or acceptable Christian doctrine. His closing lines, however, spoke volumes to seasoned and new believers alike: I'm not quite sure. But I'm going to trust, and I'm going to obey.

Daniel Towner was so struck by the power of those simple words that he quickly jotted them down, then delivered them to John Sammis, who developed the lyrics to "Trust and Obey." Towner composed the music and the song quickly became a favorite. It remains popular with hymn singers today.

Refrain:
Trust and obey, for there's no other way
To be happy in Jesus, but to trust and obey.

Verses:
When we walk with the Lord in the light of His Word,
What a glory He sheds on our way!
While we do His good will, He abides with us still,
And with all who will trust and obey.

Not a shadow can rise, not a cloud in the skies,
But His smile quickly drives it away;
Not a doubt or a fear, not a sigh or a tear,
Can abide while we trust and obey.

Not a burden we bear, not a sorrow we share,
But our toil He doth richly repay;
Not a grief or a loss, not a frown or a cross,
But is blessed if we trust and obey.

But we never can prove the delights of His love
Until all on the altar we lay;
For the favor He shows, for the joy He bestows,
Are for them who will trust and obey.

Then in fellowship sweet we will sit at His feet.
Or we'll walk by His side in the way.
What He says we will do, where He sends we will go;
Never fear, only trust and obey.

"Lord Almighty, blessed is the man who trusts in You." (Psalm 84:11-12)

Written by Connie Ruth Christiansen and included as part of the website "Sharefaith Complete Ministry Solutions." You can access this specific material at: http://www.faithclipart.com/guide/Christian-Music/hymns-the-songs-and-the-stories/trust-and-obey-the-song-and-the-story.html

Close in prayer.

Review calendar.

Assign refreshments for next week.

WEEK 6

TRUE REST GROUNDED IN THE MOST POWERFUL WEAPON IN THE COSMOS
HEBREWS 4:1-13

Opening Prayer

Group Warm-Up Question

What does it take for you to feel really rested?

Read: Hebrews 4:1-13

What important promises do we find in this passage?

This passage speaks of God's rest. Let's take a look at this concept to be sure we understand what it means.

The Scriptural Concept of "Rest" in the Past

God's Sabbath Rest

> Genesis 2:2

> Hebrews 4:4

Israel's Rest in Caanan

> Deuteronomy 12:9

> Joshua 21:43-45

> Hebrews 3:9-11

In the Present: Our Rest in Christ

> Hebrews 4:3

> Hebrews 4:7

> Matthew 11:28-30

What do you think it means when it says "take my yoke upon you?"

What are some of the characteristics of oxen in a yoke?

How do oxen in a yoke need to relate to others in their team for success in bearing their load?

How do oxen in a yoke need to relate to their master in order to have success?

Read and discuss Philippians 4:4-7 in the context of this rest and peace.

Read Hebrews 4:11-13 again and comment on the centrality of the Word of God as we claim our rest in Jesus Christ.

Future Rest: Victory in Christ

     Hebrews 4:9

     Revelation 14:13

How do we know that not everyone will experience God's rest?

Why did some of the Israelites who heard God's promise fail to receive His rest?

How does the failure of some of the Israelites to receive God's promised rest relate to us today?

How is it possible for someone today to fail to experience the rest spoken of in this passage?

Exactly how does disobedience or unbelief keep us from enjoying God's rest?

Remember from the previous discussion that noted Bible scholar Chuck Missler says that the Old Testament concept of obedience is equivalent to the New Testament concept of believing.

How would you explain Chuck Missler's statement to someone?

What kinds of things can prevent one from enjoying God's rest? (We need to avoid these things.) Please enumerate.

Read Hebrews 4:12 again.

Please list the things we learn about the Word of God in this one verse.

1.

2.

3.

4.

5.

6.

7.

Read 2 Timothy 3:16-17.

Please list the things we learn about the Word of God in this passage.

1.

2.

3.

4.

5.

6.

7.

Read Hebrews 4:13 again.

What impact does knowing that God knows everything about you (thoughts, words, actions, motivations, feelings, attitudes) have upon your life?

What impact should it have?

Application Questions

In what area of your life do you need to more fully turn things over to God?

How does the power available to us (Hebrews 4:12) relate to our need to more fully turn things over to God?

Close in prayer.

Review calendar.

Assign refreshments for next week.

WEEK 7

OUR GREAT HIGH PRIEST, YESHUA HA-MASHIACH
HEBREWS 4:14-5:10

Opening Prayer

Group Warm-Up Question

How do you normally respond to someone who gets in trouble? Why?

Read Hebrews 4:14-5:10

To what important Jewish spiritual leader did the author of Hebrews compare Jesus?

How is Jesus the ultimate High Priest?

In the Old Testament, Aaron was the first high priest. However, nobody, including Aaron, was called a Great High Priest or a Perfect High Priest. Jesus Christ is the *only* person to which this honor is accorded. Why are these special titles and the fact they apply only to Jesus Christ significant?

Read Hebrews 4:14 again.

What in particular is the writer of Hebrews encouraging the Jewish believers to do?

Read Hebrews 3:4-6 and Hebrews 3:13-15 to see the writer of Hebrews referring to this same concept.

Why do you think the early Jewish believers needed such encouragement?

Read Galatians 2:11-22 for some further insight into this.

How does this relate to us in our lives today?

In what ways did Jesus experience the same physical conditions and temptations that we do?

For some examples, read:

> John 4:6-8
>
> John 4:31
>
> Matthew 4:1-11

Were the temptations He faced equal to or greater than those that we find ourselves faced with? How so?

Why does Jesus having been tempted in this manner, as a human being, enable Him to understand our individual situation and potential temptations?

Is there a state of spiritual maturity in which supposed temptation is something against which we are protected? Can it bounce off of us like a stone bouncing off of armor?

Read Ephesians 6:10-18 and list the ingredients of an ongoing and sustained spiritual maturity that we find in these verses.

What is the difference between sinning and being tempted?

If we neglect to utilize the power available to us when tempted, does this mean that God has failed us?

Whose fault is it if we do not utilize the weapons and tools God has given us?

Read Ephesians 6:10 again.

Why do you think it is necessary for God to tell us to be strong with His mighty power when it is freely available to us?

Read Hebrews 4:16 again.

Read Exodus 25:17-22 to understand what the Israelites understood about God's throne in Israel.

Read Leviticus 16 to learn about the Day of Atonement.

Who was permitted to go before the mercy seat of God in the Old Testament?

How often was this person permitted to do this?

Understanding the background to coming before the throne of God, why was it such a huge thing for Jews to hear in Hebrews that they themselves could come before the throne.

Why is it that we can come boldly before God?

Specifically how does one approach or come before God?

What is the primary role and duty of a high priest?

Read Hebrews 5:1 again.

What characteristics make a good high priest sympathetic to those he represents?

Read Hebrews 5:2 again and explain.

How can we as modern day believers perform in a similar role?

Read Galatians 6:1 and explain.

In the Old Testament, God made provision only for people committing certain types of sin. Read:

> Exodus 21:12-14

> Numbers 15:27-31

What does this reveal to us about the character of God and the seriousness of our actions in life?

For whose sins did a high priest offer sacrifices?

Why is this significant?

Read Hebrews 5:3 again.

Read Hebrews 9:7

Who chose Israel's high priests?

How does this relate to Jesus?

Read and discuss the following verses to learn more about how this relates to Jesus:

    Hebrews 5:4-5

    Psalm 2:7

    Acts 13:32-34

Read Hebrews 5:6 again.

Who is Melchizedek? He is mentioned only two times in the Old Testament, and yet he seems to be an important figure.

Read Psalm 110:4.

Read Genesis 14:17-24.

> Notes:
>
> 1. The name Melchizedek means "King of Righteousness" and he was also the "King of Salem (peace)." (Salem was also the early name for Jerusalem.)
> 2. Jesus Christ, when He was on earth, could never have become a high priest in the normal sense since He was not a member of the tribe of Levi.
> 3. Jesus was born into the line of David, the tribe of Judah.
> 4. In the whole of Scripture, only Jesus and Melchizedek combined the offices of priest and king.

How is the position of Jesus as the Great High Priest similar to that of Melchizedek? How is it different?

Read the following verses and expand.

> Hebrews 7:1-3
>
> Hebrews 6:20-22
>
> Hebrews 7:17
>
> Hebrews 7:21
>
> Hebrews 7:23-24
>
> Hebrews 7:26-28
>
> Psalm 110:4

Similarities between Jesus and Melchizedek	Differences between Jesus and Melchizedek
1	1
2	2
3	3
4	4
5	5
6	6
7	7

Read Hebrews 5:8-9 again.

What did Jesus Christ learn from His sufferings here on earth?

How did this qualify Him as a Perfect High Priest?

How, then, did this cause Him to become "the source of eternal salvation for all who obey him?"

It sounds strange to our ears to hear that Jesus "learned obedience." When we relate this concept to Hebrews 4:14-15, we gain more insight. Jesus did not need to learn *how* to obey, but he did need to learn from personal experience what was involved for a human being to be obedient. In this way, He was and is able to be a better Perfect High Priest.

Read Matthew 26:36-46 to see the ultimate sacrifice of obedience that Jesus Christ gave.

Read 2 Corinthians 5:21 and 1 Peter 2:24 and comment on the meaning and importance of what we find there.

No one else in the history of the world died the kind of death that Jesus died. No one else suffered under the weight of the accumulated sins of mankind the way that He did.

What is the significance of the phrase "of all who obey him" in Hebrews 5:9? (NLT)

In this particular place, the concept in the Greek is tied to putting one's faith in Jesus Christ. It does not have to do with one gaining or losing salvation. Trust and obedience, which in many ways are the major theme of this book, come together in the biblical model. When one trusts, they will obey.

We also see this same phrase in the original language in:

> Acts 6:7, where it refers to a number of priests putting their faith in Christ

> Romans 10:16, where we see that not everyone put their faith in Christ

> 1 Peter 1:22, when this referred to accepting the truth of Christ

Again, we must remember that this does not in any way diminish the vital importance of living a consistent life in obedience to God and in concert with His Word. The two concepts come together. It is simply to say that in this place it is referring to the fact that once we have put our faith in Christ, and thereby obeyed His call, we experience His eternal salvation. Obedience to the Word of God in one's life on a daily basis then follows.

Why do you think suffering was part of God's will for Jesus as our high priest?

How can we honor Jesus Christ as our high priest?

Read Hebrews 5:9 again. This verse speaks of our eternal salvation. What do we learn about the purpose of our eternal salvation from the following verses?

> Ephesians 1:6
>
> Ephesians 1:12
>
> Ephesians 1:14

Application Question

What does it mean to you that Jesus faced the same type of temptations and sufferings as you?

Close in prayer.

Review calendar.

Assign refreshments for next week.

WEEK 8

WARNING AGAINST THE CONFUSING AND SUBTLE TEMPTATION TO LOSE FOCUS
HEBREWS 5:11-6:12

Opening Prayer

Group Warm-Up Question

What are some immature, childlike habits that simply would not be tolerated in an adult?

Read Hebrews 5:11-6:12

What was wrong with the group of Hebrew believers addressed in this passage?

Does Hebrews 5:11 indicate that they had developed dullness toward the Word of God?

Warren Wiersbe, in his commentary on the New Testament, says, "As we feed on the Word of God and apply it in daily life, our inner "spiritual senses" get their exercise and become strong and keen." How do you feel about his statement?

Read Hebrews 5:11-14 again.

What are some of the marks of spiritual maturity mentioned in these verses?

What, exactly, is "solid food?"

Read Hebrews 6:1-2 again.

What are some of the fundamentals of our faith?

Why is it important that believers understand these important concepts and truths?

One of the fundamentals spoken of in these verses has to do with baptism. Is this a singular or plural reference?

Most readers at first glance overlook the "s" on the end of the word baptism in this passage. While we don't have time to delve deeply into this today, it is helpful to note that there are actually seven baptisms mentioned in Scripture. At your convenience, you may wish to look these up and engage in some further study. The seven baptisms found in Scripture follow.

1. The baptism of Israel on a national or corporate basis—1491 BC (Exodus 14)

2. The baptism under law or unto repentance, which also called the baptism of John (John the Baptist)—30 AD (Matthew 3, Mark 1, Luke 3, John 1)

3. The baptism of Jesus Christ in death—33 AD (Matthew 27, Mark 15, Luke 23, John 19)

4. Jewish baptism—33 AD (Acts 2)

5. Gentile baptism—41 AD (Acts 10)

6. The baptism of the Holy Spirit, the one true baptism at the moment one is regenerated whether one is Jew or Gentile (1 Corinthians 12)

7. The baptism of fire (Matthew 3, Revelation 20)

Having gone over this list, we should note quite specifically that there are seven (7) baptisms that we can find in Scripture. The number 7 appears significant in the Word of God at important times and places. To the best of your knowledge, what is the significance of this number as it relates to God and Scripture?

This study of the number 7 in Scripture is, again, another topic that opens itself up to some fascinating and in-depth study. It behooves all of us to take the time to understand and study this. At the same time, this also shows us the depth of the topics covered in Hebrews. The author has in many ways wrapped up the whole of Scripture as succinctly as possible for his Jewish audience. (In short, the number seven signifies completeness.)

Read Hebrews 6:3 again.

What should be the ongoing result of our spiritual growth?

Read 1 Timothy 4:7-8 and expand upon this.

Read Hebrews 6:4-6 again.

This has been a difficult passage for many people over the years. First, we must remember to whom this was written. Read Hebrews 3:1 to see this.

This is thus not a salvation passage; it is speaking to the issue of making our lives fruitful and useful. This is also quite evident when examining Hebrews 6:4-6 in the Greek.

For a discussion and examination of this as it relates to the Greek, consider the following:

There are five characteristics of the people listed in Hebrews 6:4-6. They:

1. Are once enlightened
2. Have experienced the good things of heaven
3. Have shared in the Holy Spirit
4. Have tasted the goodness of the Word of God
5. Have tasted of prophecy and the power of the age to come

When we tear this apart in the Greek, we find that the word "enlightened" used in verse 4 is the Greek word *photizo,* which means "to make see." It is also the origin of the English word photograph, photo, and photography. This same word is used in Ephesians 1:18, Hebrews 10:32, and John 3:3, where it says in the NLT:

I pray that your hearts will be flooded with light so that you can understand the wonderful future he has promised to those he called. I want you to realize what a rich and glorious inheritance he has given to his people. (Ephesians 1:18)

> Remember those earlier days after you had received the light, when you stood your ground in a great contest in the face of suffering. (Hebrews 10:32)

> Jesus replied, "I assure you, unless you are born again, you can never see the Kingdom of God." (John 3:3)

These people have experienced the second birth through Jesus Christ.

Next, if we examine the word "tasted" in Hebrews 6:5, we find the Greek word *genomai*. This implies a total experience. We can see how this implies such an all-consuming and total experience when we see it also appearing in Hebrews 2:9.

> What we do see is Jesus, who "for a little while was made lower than the angels" and now is "crowned with glory and honor" because he suffered death for us. Yes, by God's grace, Jesus tasted death for everyone in all the world.

In the same way that Jesus experienced death on our behalf, these people have had the fully consuming experience of a life in Christ.

If we then also examine the word for partakers, or those who have shared in the Holy Spirit, we find the Greek word *metochos,* which means a totally involving relationship of sharing to the fullest extent. We also see this word translated 5 times as partakers in the King James Version.

> Wherefore, holy brethren, partakers of the heavenly calling, consider the Apostle and High Priest of our profession, Christ Jesus… (Hebrews 3:1)

> For we are made partakers of Christ, if we hold the beginning of our confidence steadfast unto the end… (Hebrews 3:14)

For *it is* impossible for those who were once enlightened, and have tasted of the heavenly gift, and were made partakers of the Holy Ghost, (Hebrews 6:4)

But if ye be without chastisement, whereof all are partakers, then are ye bastards, and not sons. (Hebrews 12:8)

For they verily for a few days chastened us after their own pleasure; but he for our profit, that we might be partakers of his holiness. (Hebrews 12:10)

It may also be helpful to view these same verses in the New Living Translation.

And so, dear brothers and sisters who belong to God and are bound for heaven think about this Jesus whom we declare to be God's Messenger and High Priest. (Hebrews 3:1)

For if we are faithful to the end, trusting God just as firmly as when we first believed, we will share in all that belongs to Christ. (Hebrews 3:14)

For it is impossible to bring back to repentance those who were once enlightened— those who have experienced the good things of heaven and shared in the Holy Spirit, (Hebrews 6:4)

If God doesn't discipline you as he does all of his children, it means that you are illegitimate and are not really his children at all. (Hebrews 12:8)

For our earthly fathers disciplined us for a few years, doing the best they knew how. But God's discipline is always right and good for us because it means we will share in his holiness. (Hebrews 12:10)

This same Greek word, *metochos*, is translated as "fellows" in Hebrews 1:9 in the King James Version and then again as partakers in 1 Corinthians 9:10, 2 Timothy 2:6, 1 Corinthians 10:17, 1 Peter 4:13, and 2 Peter 1:4.

Thou hast loved righteousness, and hated iniquity; therefore God, even thy God, hath anointed thee with the oil of gladness above thy fellows. (Hebrews 1:9)

Or saith he it altogether for our sakes? For our sakes, no doubt, this is written: that he that ploweth should plow in hope; and that he that thresheth in hope should be partaker of his hope. (1 Corinthians 9:10)

The husbandman that laboureth must be first partaker of the fruits. (2 Timothy 2:6)

For we being many are one bread, and one body: for we are all partakers of that one bread. (1 Corinthians 10:17)

But rejoice, inasmuch as ye are partakers of Christ's sufferings; that, when his glory shall be revealed, ye may be glad also with exceeding joy. (1 Peter 4:13)

Whereby are given unto us exceeding great and precious promises: that by these ye might be partakers of the divine nature, having escaped the corruption that is in the world through lust. (2 Peter 1:4)

As before, it may also be helpful to view these verses in the New Living Translation.

You love what is right and hate what is wrong. Therefore God, your God, has anointed you, pouring out the oil of joy on you more than on anyone else. (Hebrews 1:9)

Wasn't he also speaking to us? Of course he was. Just as farm workers who plow fields and thresh the grain expect a share of the harvest, Christian workers should be paid by those they serve. (1 Corinthians 9:10)

Hardworking farmers are the first to enjoy the fruit of their labor. (2 Timothy 2:6)

And we all eat from one loaf, showing that we are one body. (1 Corinthians 10:17)

Instead, be very glad—because these trials will make you partners with Christ in his suffering, and afterward you will have the wonderful joy of sharing his glory when it is displayed to all the world. (1 Peter 4:13)

And by that same mighty power, he has given us all of his rich and wonderful promises. He has promised that you will escape the decadence all around you caused by evil desires and that you will share in his divine nature. (2 Peter 1:4)

These verses certainly seem to indicate that these people were sharing in a personal relationship with Jesus Christ to the fullest extent.

In addition, we must understand the context in which this was written. In the New Testament we are constantly warned to not rely upon the law for our salvation. In the case of Jewish believers, this concern is even greater in that they previously did rely upon the law to be put right with God. They are warned to not drift away and return to a legalistic system of justification before God when they have enjoyed the results of faith and God's grace. We can see this at work in the following passages:

Hebrews 2:1

Hebrews 3:12-14

Romans 10:1-5

Romans 6:4-6

Galatians 3:1-11

If we then follow the thread of this argument to the end of today's passage, we end up at Hebrews 6:11-12. (Read these two verses again.)

Here we see a reference to our inheritance. Remember, this was written to believers and they were being encouraged to be sure they received their rewards and inheritance.

Read 1 Corinthians 9:24-27.

Who were the other people in this race with Paul?

Answer: Believers

Paul was worried about being fruitful. He wanted to be sure that he lived his life in such a way as to receive the rewards available to him as the result of a dynamic righteous life.

Read and explain the following verses as they relate to this concept.

> 1 Corinthians 3:11-15
>
> 2 Timothy 1:9-12

One must be extra cautious to not be caught up in the legalism that was so tempting to the Jews. Indeed, we see this same temptation to legalism and justifying ourselves through our own efforts in Catholicism and some protestant denominations. The problem that arises from this incorrect construct is that a person may repeatedly and continually lose their salvation and then need to again "be saved." They go to the priest or the altar and "become believers again."

These unfortunate people, trapped in this never-ending cycle of sin/salvation, sin/salvation, sin/salvation, sin/salvation, can never really grow. This is exactly the type of problem being encountered in the first century, as we see when we read Hebrews 5:11-14.

Having said all of this, it is vitally important that we do not become complacent in our relationship with God. The fact that we are saved God's by grace does not mean that that we can sit on our couches and let the world go by, acting as one wishes, feeling that all one may lose is their inheritance or rewards. If one feels and acts that way, it is *prima facie* evidence that they have not experienced the life-changing faith offered by Jesus Christ. Such a person must attend to their relationship with God and be sure that they are indeed a believer experiencing the fruit of the Spirit in their lives and living in a fashion that pleases God on a daily basis.

Read the following verses and expand upon this:

James 2:17-20

James 2:26

Read Hebrews 6:7 again.

What is the result of a believer living a life of maturity and obedience?

Read Hebrews 6:8 again.

What is the result when one is not mature, consistent and obedient to the will of God as revealed in the Scriptures?

In reading the second half of this verse, does it appear that one might lose their rewards?

Read Hebrews 3:15-19.

How does the concept of hardening one's heart relate to this?

Is the hardening of one's heart generally due to one life-altering decision to turn from God, or is it a gradual thing?

Remember: The Greek word for such hardening is *sklerotes*. This means a gradual and continual hardening. The word *sklerotes* is also the root of the English word "arteriosclerosis," which refers to a gradual and continual hardening of the arteries.

Why do people sometimes fall victim to this gradual hardening?

How does this impact them in a spiritual sense in everyday life?

How does this impact them in an emotional way in everyday life?

How does this impact them in a sense of conscious awareness in everyday life?

How does this impact them in a practical sense in everyday life?

What effect does this have on the peace and contentment one may or may not feel on a daily basis?

Read Hebrews 6:9-10 again.

What important points does the Holy Spirit want us to realize by placing these two verses after the warnings graciously given to us in our study so far?

Read Hebrews 6:10 again.

What does it show to each other and to the world at large when believers properly care for and help each other?

Read Hebrews 6:12 again.

What happens when a person falls away and what are the further consequences of this gradual process?

Do you agree that falling away is a gradual process?

What great promise do we have if we persevere in our commitment to Christ?

Read Proverbs 24:30-34.

How might one apply the principles in these verses to our lives in a spiritual sense?

Application Questions

What decisions are you facing in your life right now that require extra discernment?

What steps can you take to be sure that the decisions you make will be pleasing to God?

Close in prayer.

Review calendar.

Assign refreshments for next time.

WEEK 9

ABSOLUTE SECURITY AND CONFIDENCE IN THE PROMISES OF GOD
HEBREWS 6:13-20

Opening Prayer

Group Warm-Up Question

What gives you personally a sense of security?

Read Hebrews 6:13-20

What promise did God make to Abraham?

Read Genesis 22:16-17.

Read Hebrews 6:13-14 again.

How does this tie in with what we learned in Hebrews 6:10-12?

How do faith and patience contrast with dullness, slothfulness and indifference?

Read Hebrews 12:1-2 to see what the author of Hebrews encourages the "Jewish Christians" to do in the face of temptation to fall back into the comfortable, familiar, and yet dead practices of Judaism without Jesus.

Are people today ever faced with a similar temptation? When and how?

To see what Jesus had to say about this, read and discuss Matthew 13:3-23.

Specifically, how do you relate this to what we just read in Hebrews 12:1-2?

How did Abraham respond to God's promise?

Read Hebrews 6:15 again.

What was the result of Abraham's response to God's promise?

Read Romans 4:1-5 and discuss another important aspect of Abraham's patience.

What else do we learn about patience in the Scriptures?

Think about the source of patience, the learning of patience, and the result of patience.

Read the following verses and list what we learn about this important evidence of God working in one's life:

Ecclesiastes 7:8

Romans 2:4

Romans 9:22

2 Corinthians 6:6

Galatians 5:22-23

Ephesians 4:2

Colossians 1:11

Colossians 3:12-13

1 Timothy 1:15-16

1 Timothy 3:10

James 5:10

Hebrews 6:12

Qualities of Patience

1.

2.

3.

4.

5.

6.

7.

What do we learn about oaths in Hebrews 6:16?

What else do we learn about oaths in Scripture?

Read the following verses and note what we learn. In particular, pay attention to the seriousness of oaths and who should or should not be taking or making oaths.

Deuteronomy 7:8

Deuteronomy 9:5

Genesis 26:3

Leviticus 5:4

Ecclesiastes 8:2

Hosea 4:15

Numbers 30:2

Nehemiah 10:29

Acts 2:30

Acts 23:12

Acts 23:14

Hebrews 7:20

Hebrews 7:21

Hebrews 7:28

James 5:12

Matthew 5:33-37

Exodus 20:7

Oaths

1.

2.

3.

4.

5.

6.

7.

Why did God bind himself with an oath?

Read Hebrews 6:17 again.

What is a promise?

Read the following verses and explain the import of the promises we see recorded. Pay particular attention to the person making the promise and the reliability of the promise.

Psalm 119:57

Genesis 28:15

Numbers 10:29

Deuteronomy 26:16-29

1 Kings 8:56

Joshua 21:45

Acts 2:33

Acts 13:23

Ephesians 3:6

Romans 1:2

What is the difference between an oath and a promise?

Read the following verses in which both a promise and an oath are mentioned in close proximity to one another. How do these two concepts interact?

Nehemiah 5:12

Hebrews 6:17

The Merriam Webster online dictionary defines a promise as

"1 *a* :a declaration that one will do or refrain from doing something specified *b* :a legally binding declaration that gives the person to whom it is made a right to expect or to claim the performance or forbearance of a specified act."

Merriam Webster also defines an oath as "*a (1)* :a solemn usually formal calling upon God or a god to witness to the truth of what one says or to witness that one sincerely intends to do what one says *(2)* :a solemn attestation of the truth or inviolability of one's words." "*b* :something (as a promise) corroborated by an oath."

Read Hebrews 6:18 again.

Why did God use both an oath and a promise? What is the significance of this?

We know from Scripture, history, and experience that God's promises are absolutely true. God always keeps His promises. However, to drive this home to human beings, He has combined his promises with an oath. We see from this that nothing in this world is more certain than the promises of God and our security in Him.

God's promise and His oath are to the heirs of God's promise. To whom does this refer in a spiritual sense? Read the following verses and explain:

Hebrews 6:17

Hebrews 11:9

Galatians 3:29

Hebrews 6:18 also speaks about "our refuge." This is a serious and important concept from the Old Testament that was very clear to the Jewish believers of the time. Read the following verses to learn about the concept of refuge:

> Numbers 35
>
> Deuteronomy 19:1-20
>
> Joshua 20

Do you think it is correct to say that "Jesus is our refuge"? How so?

Read Hebrews 7:23-25 and comment.

What do we learn about the biblical concept of hope as it applies to us in Hebrews 6:19?

How would you describe the certainty that you have in Jesus Christ to a friend?

The Greek philosopher Epictetus wrote, "One must not tie a ship to a single anchor, nor life to a single hope." How does this contrast to what believers have in Jesus Christ?

It is also interesting to note that the anchor was a common and precious symbol to the early believers. Indeed, over sixty-five drawings of anchors have been found in the Roman catacombs.

Read the following two verses and explain what they mean in the light of this concept.

> Colossians 1:5

> 1 Timothy 1:1

What is the difference between an earthly anchor and being anchored in Jesus Christ? Please list several. (Hint: One keeps you in place while the other keeps you secure while enabling you to move ahead.)

Read Hebrews 6:19 again.

What does it mean that our trust in Christ leads us through the veil into God's inner sanctuary?

Read the following verses to help us gain an understanding of this concept:

> Hebrews 9:1-12

> Hebrews 10:19-22

Read Matthew 27:46-53 to see the exact moment in human history when this was accomplished.

This rending of the veil was a momentous event. Early Jewish literature generally indicates that this veil was as "thick as a man's hand," or supposedly about 4-6 inches (depending upon the man) and so heavy and cumbersome that it required 300 priests to wash it. Assuming these descriptions to be accurate, this rending of the veil was impossible by human standards.

At The Tabernacle Place, which can be accessed at the-tabernacle-place.com, we find the following statement:

> "So the presence of God remained shielded from man behind a thick curtain during the history of Israel. However, Jesus' sacrificial death on the cross changed that. When He died, the curtain in the Jerusalem temple was torn in half, from the top to the bottom. Only God could have carried out such an incredible feat because the veil was too high for human hands to have reached it, and too thick to have torn it. (The Jerusalem temple, a replica of the wilderness tabernacle, had a curtain that was about 60 feet in height, 30 feet in width and four inches thick.) Furthermore, it was torn from top down, meaning this act must have come from above."

Read Hebrews 6:20 again.

Here we again encounter Melchizedek. Yeshua Ha-Mashiach, the Jewish Messiah, became our eternal high priest in the order of Melchizedek. As such, He leads us into a relationship with God. The whole Levitical system which we find in the Old Testament is involved in this statement. The Jewish readers at the time realized that this entire system, with its veil and High Priest, was a forerunner of Jesus Christ. It was prophecy encoded in a system of regular practice. When one understands it as the Scripturally literate Jews of the time did, we come to realize that it all points to the Messiah. In fact, many competent biblical scholars contend that one can find Jesus Christ on every page of the Old Testament, and especially in the five books of Moses.

How can a believer express their confidence in God's promises in everyday life?

Read the following verses and discuss how the things they mention show that a person has this surety and confidence in the promises of God.

1 Corinthians 16:13-14

Ephesians 4:29-30

Ephesians 5:15-16

Philippians 2:14-16

Colossians 3:23-24

Application Questions

How does it impact your life on a day to day basis when you realize that God gives every believer an eternal and secure inheritance in heaven?

In what area of your life do you need to follow Abraham's example of patience?

Close in prayer.

Review calendar.

Assign refreshments for next time.

WEEK 10

MELCHIZEDEK RETURNS
HEBREWS 7:1-10

Opening Prayer

Group Warm-Up Question

What person from history do you most admire? Why?

Just as Arnold Schwarzeneger uttered his infamous phrase "I'll be back" in the first Terminator movie, Melchizedek is back. In fact, not only is he back, but the fact that he keeps coming to the fore in the book of Hebrews indicates that we have some relatively important things to learn through him. The writer of Hebrews made some important points in the discussion about Melchizedek in the fourth chapter of the book. Here he expands upon that foundation in some surprising ways. And yet in the future we will see Melchizedek again as the Holy Spirit continues to teach us through this personage.

In fact, as one views the whole of Hebrews, we can see God carefully laying out the logical progression of His plan. We can see the patterns, promises, and predictions of the Jewish Tanakh, which Gentiles call the Old Testament, come to fruition in Yeshua Ha-Mashiach, the Jewish Messiah. Today, we know Him as Jesus Christ.

Read Hebrews 7:1-10

Let's start this session like a crime scene investigation. Let's just start with the facts. For those of us who once saw the television series "Dragnet," or perhaps the movie, we might remember how Officer Friday began a case. He would ask for the facts, saying when someone tried to embellish a story, "Just the facts, ma'am."

To get to those facts, let's answer a series of questions together. Doing so will help clarify our thinking and understanding of the issues being addressed. The answers are in the text, so our job is easier than that of Officer Friday.

Who was Melchizedek?

How was Melchizedek associated with Abraham?

What did Abraham give to Melchizedek?

What does the name Melchizedek mean?

What is significant about the title "King of Salem?"

What thing about Melchizedek's life that we see in Genesis foreshadowed the priesthood of Jesus Christ?

What about Melchizedek shows us his greatness?

How did the Mosaic Law provide for the Levitical priests in the Old Testament?

What was so unusual about Abraham giving a tithe to Melchizedek?

What does the long-standing practice of one person blessing another say about the position of the two parties involved?

How did the tithe collected by Melchizedek differ from all of the other tithes collected by the Levitical priests in the time after Melchizedek?

How is it possible that Levi, who was as yet unborn, paid tithes to Melchizedek?

Now that we have concluded the initial fact finding part of our investigation, let's examine what it means. In order to do this, we need to first read Genesis 14:17-24 and combine this with what we already read in Hebrews 7:1-10. In these passages, we find a number of important points that we need to understand.

1. Melchizedek was both a king and a priest.

   In the Old Testament the offices of king and priest were always separated, except in this one singular instance. Not even Aaron, the first high priest under the Levitical system, had this distinction.

2. The name of Melchizedek is very important.

    Today many people give their children names without any real significance in relationship to what they mean. Witness the many strange names you hear in today's society. In the time the Bible was written, names were sometimes changed when a great event or crisis occurred. Read Genesis 32:24-32 and John 1:35-42 to see this.

    In Hebrew, the name Melchizedek means "king of righteousness." Melchizedek is the king of Salem. The word in Hebrew for Salem is *Shalom*, which means peace. Melchizedek's name therefore means "king of righteousness and king of peace." In the Scriptures, we often find righteousness and peace together.

    Read the following verses to see how this interaction works. It is particularly helpful to see these verses in several translations. One of them needs to be the King James Version to get the full importance and flavor of what is being said.

    Isaiah 32:17

    Psalm 85:10

    Psalm 72:7

    James 3:17-18

    Hebrews 12:10-11

    Romans 5:1 and Galatians 2:21 Together

    John 14:27

Jesus Christ offers inner peace. How does this tie in with righteousness in our day-to-day existence?

3. Melchizedek's family history is different.

In order for someone to serve as a priest under the Levitical system, it was necessary for them to prove their ancestry. We can see this in Ezra 2:61-63 and Nehemiah 7:63-65.

As far as the record is concerned, Melchizedek was not born, nor did he die. In this way he was a picture of Jesus Christ, the eternal Son of God (see Hebrews 7:3).

Since there is no record of Melchizedek's death, he is, in a sense, still serving as a king and a priest, and is in this way like Jesus Christ (see Hebrews 7:16).

Melchizedek was, however, a real person: a man, a king, and a priest. He was not an Old Testament appearance of Jesus Christ. He was here on the earth serving in the functions described in the Scriptures. The fact that Melchizedek essentially held down two important and ongoing jobs differentiates him from any other events that we see as Old Testament appearances of Jesus. In every other instance where we see Christ appearing in the Old Testament, He is there, without a job or ongoing function, and then He is gone. This distinction in and of itself would seem to disqualify Melchizedek as what is sometimes referred to as a "Christophany." While it does not appear that this was such an event, Melchizedek is still a vitally important person with a vitally important role as a picture of the Messiah who was to come.

What does it mean in your life that Jesus Christ is both a king and a priest?

What does it mean to you that Jesus Christ is both the King and the High Priest *forever?*

4. Melchizedek had the authority to receive tithes and to give blessings.

   Read Hebrews 7:4-8 again to remind ourselves of the import of this.

   What is the significance of Levi's descendants paying a tithe to Melchizedek?

   How does the authority of Melchizedek to receive tithes and give blessings then relate to Jesus Christ?

Application Question

In this study we have seen the exalted nature of Jesus Christ as our Priest and King.

What can you do this week to more fully realize and experience your security as you enjoy your relationship with Him?

Assignment for Next Time

In order to make the next lesson more meaningful, I recommend everyone read Leviticus 8 and Leviticus 9 before our next meeting.

Close in prayer

Review calendar

Assign refreshments for next time.

WEEK 11

A MOMENTOUS CHANGE
HEBREWS 7:11-28

Opening Prayer

This study brings us to a momentous declaration in the book of Hebrews. The author has been carefully laying the foundation for the direct statements that are about to be made. One logical point backed by the Old Testament Scriptures has been built upon another to get to this juncture where the undeniable conclusion about a major change in Judaism is explained.

This change is more major than most modern day readers can fathom. For centuries, the tribe of Levi served as priests according to the plan of God. Now we have the announcement that this priesthood has ended. The writer of Hebrews explains this by showing that the order of Melchizedek is superior to and replaces the priesthood of the Levites, which originated with Aaron. This turned the whole system of their relationship with God on its head and was difficult for Jews to accept and explain. That is, it was somewhat difficult until they read Hebrews, where God clearly laid it out for them.

In one sense, this was the end of the line for them. In yet another sense, this was the fulfillment of all of the Old Testament prophecies in the person of Jesus Christ, Yeshua Ha-Mashiach, the Jewish Messiah. It was at the same time exciting, exhilarating, and frightening. For those in love with the religiosity of the old system and with their place in it, it was too upsetting to accept. This was in spite of the undeniable truths of Scripture and their fulfillment before their eyes. For others with the courage, desire, and honesty to follow hard after God, it was a new beginning.

Group Warm-Up Questions

When might a person want to be represented by a lawyer?

Why might a person need this representation?

Read Hebrews 7:11-28

Here we see that not only is Melchizedek greater than Aaron, he has replaced Aaron. It is no longer the order of Levi or Aaron, it is the order of Melchizedek.

What does a new priesthood require?

Why was it necessary for God to institute such a radical change?

Read the following references and explain:

>Hebrews 7:11-14

>Hebrews 7:19

>Hebrews 10:1-3

"Perfect" and "perfection" are key words in the book of Hebrews. In the context of the book and in the Greek they mean "completed and fulfilled." Read the following verses and comment on perfection, especially as it relates to the meaning in Greek.

>Hebrews 2:10

>Hebrews 5:9

>Hebrews 6:1

>Hebrews 7:11

>Hebrews 7:19

>Hebrews 9:9

>Hebrews 10:1

>Hebrews 10:14

>Hebrews 7:28

What, then, was the purpose of the Mosaic law?

Read Galatians 3:19-4:7 and explain.

From what tribe did Jesus come?

What connection did Jesus' tribe have to the Jewish priesthood?

Read Hebrews 7:14 again for help.

By what mechanism did Jesus become a priest?

Read Hebrews 7:15-16 to help you construct an answer.

How is the new covenant superior to the old system of priesthood and law?

Read Hebrews 7:18-19.

The law of Moses made no provision for a high priest from the tribe of Judah (see Hebrews 7:14). Since our High Priest is from the tribe of Judah, there had to have been a change in the law of Moses. There has now been such a change. This occurred when the entire system of Old Testament law was fulfilled in Jesus Christ. Read the following verses and comment:

    Colossians 2:13-14

    Galatians 5:1-6

    Romans 7:1-4

Does this freedom from the law mean that a believer may now be lawless?

Does being "free from the law" equate to being "free to sin?"

How and why do believers both trust and obey God? Read the following verses and comment:

> 2 Corinthians 5:14

> Ephesians 6:6

> Romans 8:1-4

Read Hebrews 7:15-19 again.

The word "another" in Hebrews 7:15 (KJV) means "another of a different kind."

Why could the old law not continue?

What do we find out about the nature of Christ and the change He has bought about in Hebrews 7:16? Please explain.

How is Jesus Christ unique in comparison to the other priests who represented Israel before God?

Read Hebrews 7:17 again.

Read Hebrews 7:23-28 again.

List the ways in which Jesus Christ, the Jewish Messiah, is unique as a priest.

1.

2.

3.

4.

5.

6.

7.

What does this passage say to those who feel the need for a human priest?

How does Christ's priesthood give us confidence to approach God?

From whence did the priests receive their authority?

Read Hebrews 7:28 and explain.

Hebrews 7:18 refers to the actual annulling or abolishment of the Old Testament priesthood. This is a momentous moment in history.

The Duties and Symbolism of a Levitical High Priest

Even though Jesus is now our High Priest, it is helpful to realize that every aspect of the Levitical or Aaronic priesthood points to the coming Perfect High Priest and Messiah, Jesus Christ. A summary of Leviticus 8 and 9 in relationship to the rest of the Scriptures shows some important things that we should be sure to understand. These include:

1. While Jesus was not born into the Levitical priesthood, every detail of that system points to Him.

2. In Leviticus, we find the concept of genealogy. It was important to establish Jesus' position in the line of Melchizedek.

3. The high priests were washed and anointed. The concept of the water and the Word of God are linked. We are "washed in His blood" once in a judicial sense and we must be washed daily and continually by His Word.

4. Jesus' baptism was not for the forgiveness of any sins. It was a symbolic washing following the pattern of Leviticus 8. His ministry began with the symbolic ceremonial washing seen in the Aaronic priesthood and reflected in His baptism. This was a matter of fulfillment as the ultimate High Priest began His ministry.

5. The details of the priests are all significant.

   • They were clothed in white garments, a symbol of righteousness.
   • They made a sin offering pointing ultimately to Jesus.
   • They put blood on their right ear to cover what they heard from sin.
   • They put blood on their right foot to cover them from sin where they went.
   • They put blood on their right thumb to cover what they did from sin.
   • They were anointed with sacred oil, a symbol of the Holy Spirit.
   • The sacred oil itself was incredibly expensive, as is the sacrifice of Christ which ultimately brought the anointing of the Holy Spirit.

6. The offerings of the high priests didn't really pay for sins. They were a foreshadowing of Jesus Christ, the only one with the ability to pay for sin.

   • Offerings actually began prior to their institutionalization in Leviticus. Note that Abraham (Genesis 22), Cain, and Abel all made offerings. Even at these early stages, these offerings were a foreshadowing of Christ.
   • Isaiah 53 shows the coming Jewish Messiah as the one who can and will pay for sins.

7. The clothing of the high priest was also significant.

   • The high priest wore a seamless robe.
   • Jesus wore a seamless white robe.

- The concept of being clothed in white linen or righteousness is also seen throughout Revelation in verses 3: 4-6; 7:13-17 and 15:6 among others.
- The high priest also wore a golden girdle or sash while performing his duties; Jesus is likewise shown as wearing a golden girdle or sash in the book of Revelation (1:13).
- The high priest wore a breastplate with 12 precious stones; we also see these same stones in Revelation 21:18, but in a different order, perhaps to symbolize Jesus' role as the High Priest, but in the order of Melchizedek.

Jesus Christ is our High Priest in the order of Melchizedek. Every detail of the Levitical priesthood points to Him and His role as a spotless sacrifice. He could actually accomplish what the high priests in the order of Aaron could only hint at. His office is perpetual, non-transferable, and does not expire.

The Ultimate Call of the Book of Hebrews

The book of Hebrews is a call to Jewish believers to come out of the ritualism and chains of Judaism to the new life and rest afforded to them by God in the person of His Son. It is, therefore, a call to maturity as they realize the culmination of the practices and patterns of Judaism are fulfilled in Jesus Christ. At the heart of this maturity is obedience.

Read Mark 16:15-16.

What was the focus of the command Jesus gave to his disciples in this passage?

What did he want people to do?

Read Mathew 28:18-20.

What important augmentation do we see in these verses as they relate to Mark 16:15-16?

Why is simply believing not enough for a believer in order to live a victorious life?

Read the following references from Hebrews to see how God was calling the believing Jews to do the same thing Jesus commanded the disciples to tell people to do:

> Hebrews 5:12

> Hebrews 6:1

Application Question

How can the fact that Jesus is our Great High Priest enable you to live a life that is pleasing to God this week?

Assignment for next time

We need two class members to volunteer to read, study, and report on one of the following books:

1. *God's Appointed Times* by Barry Kasdan.
2. *Christ in the Passover* by Moishe and Ceil Rosen.

Close in prayer.

Review calendar.

Assign refreshments for next time.

WEEK 12

THE HIGH PRIEST OF A BETTER COVENANT EXACTLY AS FORETOLD
HEBREWS 8:1-13

Opening Prayer

Group Warm-Up Question

Name some items in your office or home that have become obsolete.

Why have these particular things become out of date or been put aside?

Read Hebrews 8:1-13

Read Hebrews 8:1-3 again.

According to this passage, where is our High Priest right now?

How is our High Priest spending his time?

In reading Hebrews 8:3, it is very important to note that the tense of the word for offering in Greek is singular. This tense implies that the "offering was once and for all." Please read Hebrews 9:24-28 for a clarification of this concept.

We see clearly that Christ is "a living sacrifice" in heaven. He is not offering himself over and over, as this is not necessary. He offered Himself as the one sacrifice for sin forever.

Read Hebrews 8:4-6 again.

Why did the writer say that if Jesus Christ were on earth, he would not be a priest?

What was the difference between what the priests on earth were doing as compared to what our great High Priest was and is doing?

Why, then, is the job given to our High Priest so much superior to that of the priests who served under the old laws?

Read Exodus 25:40.

Why was it so vitally important that everything in the place of worship was done in exact accordance with the instructions the Israelites received from God?

What vital truths is God communicating to us in this verse?

How is it possible that our High Priest *guarantees a better covenant with God, based on better promises?*

This new covenant was spoken of many years before.

Read Jeremiah 31:31-34 to see this being introduced overtly to the Jewish people.

Read 2 Corinthians 3 to see the new covenant in contrast to the old.

At your convenience you may also wish to read Galatians 3 and 4 to see this in greater detail. The writer of Hebrews also continues to expound upon this theme in Hebrews 9 and 12, as we will see in subsequent sessions.

In what great ways does the new covenant differ from the old? List as many of these differences as possible.

New Covenant	Old Covenant
1.	1.
2.	2.
3.	3.
4.	4.
5.	5.
6.	6.
7.	7.

8.	8.
9.	9.
10.	10.

This brings us to some important discoveries about the supernatural nature of Scripture and the nature of God. In our studies prior to this, we have occasionally said that if one looks closely, they "find Jesus Christ on every page of the Old Testament." Let us now examine some supernatural ways in which God did just this in His Word, even though the participants at the time may not have been fully aware of what was going on. This is probably most readily apparent in the five books of Moses, where everything is a foreshadowing of the Jewish Messiah, whom we know as Jesus Christ.

Read Matthew 5:17-18 to see what our Jewish Messiah had to say about this.

Also read the following verses to see this corroborated:

     Romans 15:4

     Colossians 2:16-17

In order to get a good overview of this, we will now listen to the report on *God's Appointed Times* by Barry Kasdan. Rose Publishing also produces a helpful and interesting fold out chart on this material. Every class member should obtain a copy of this information to review on their own.

We would do well to remember that, to the Western mind, prophecy entails prediction and fulfillment. At the same time, the Jewish mind takes this a step further in that prophecy also includes specific and meaningful patterns.

I also recommend that everyone obtain and study a copy of the book, *Christ in the Passover* by Moishe Rosen. The Passover is the Jewish feast that Jesus Christ himself celebrated at what we call the Last Supper. This Old Testament feast points to Jesus Christ in every way.

One of the most meaningful experiences a believer can have is to attend a Messianic Passover Seder. As we noted, this is the feast Jesus celebrated at the Last Supper. I recommend that every believer take part in such an event if they have the opportunity. This experience imbues an even greater sense of supernatural awe when conducted by a Messianic Jewish Rabbi.

Most amazingly, the particulars of the sacrifice of Jesus Christ were foretold quite specifically in other places in the Old Testament.

Read Psalm 22 to see a description of the crucifixion of Christ before crucifixion was even invented.

Read Isaiah 53 to again see a description of the sacrifice of Yeshua Ha-Mashiach.

It is undeniable that these prophecies were fulfilled in the person of Jesus Christ to anyone who has a good working knowledge of history.

And to make this even more interesting, at your convenience take a look at the description and analysis of the camp of Israel from the Old Testament at the end of this lesson.

Read Hebrews 8:7-12 again.

Why was there a need for a new covenant?

Does this mean that God made some sort of a mistake with the old covenant?

Read Exodus 19:8 and Exodus 24:3.

How did the ancient Israelites first respond to God's old covenant?

In reading Hebrews 8:8, we must be sure to not fall into error by incorrectly allegorizing and concluding that the church is "the spiritual Israel." Once we make the illogical jump to make such plain words as Judah and Israel mean something else, there is no end to the errors one may introduce in their study of Scripture. As in our study on Romans, it would behoove us to again review the following principles on "How to Avoid Error" as we study God's Word.

How to Avoid Error

(Partially excerpted from *The Road to Holocaust* by Hal Lindsey)

1. The most important single principle in determining the true meaning of any doctrine of our faith is that we start with the clear statements of the Scriptures that specifically apply to it, and use those to interpret the parables, allegories, and obscure passages. This allows Scripture to interpret Scripture. The Dominionists (and others seeking to bend Scripture to suit their purposes) frequently reverse this order, seeking to interpret the clear passages using obscure passages, parables, and allegories.

2. The second most important principle is to consistently interpret by the literal, grammatical, historical method. This means the following:

   a. Each word should be interpreted in light of its normal, ordinary usage that was accepted in the times in which it was written.

   b. Each sentence should be interpreted according to the rules of grammar and syntax normally accepted when the document was written.

   c. Each passage should also be interpreted in light of its historical and cultural environment.

Most false doctrines and heresy of Church history can be traced to a failure to adhere to these principles. Church history is filled with examples of disasters and wrecked lives wrought by men failing to base their doctrine, faith, and practice upon these two principles.

The Reformation, more than anything else, was caused by an embracing of the literal, grammatical, and historical method of interpretation, and a discarding of the allegorical method. The allegorical system had veiled the Church's understanding of many vital truths for nearly a thousand years.

It is important to note that this is how Jesus interpreted Scripture. He interpreted literally, grammatically, and recognized double reference in prophecy. It is likewise important that we view Scripture as a whole. Everything we read in God's Word is part of a cohesive, consistent, integrated message system. Every part of Scripture fits in perfectly with the whole of Scripture if we read, understand, and study it properly.

Remember to appropriate the power of the Holy Spirit.

Read the following verses:

Luke 11:11-13

1 Timothy 4:15-16

Luke 24:49

2 Peter 2:1

John 7:39

Mark 13:22

John 14:14-17

John 14: 26

Read Hebrews 8:9 again.

After their first response to God's old covenant, how did the Israelites perform?

Is it possible that God foreknew how the Israelites (and we) would respond to the old covenant and planned His response before the people involved were even born?

Read the following verses and comment.

Ecclesiastes 3:11

Isaiah 41:26

Isaiah 46:10

Isaiah 48:3

Read Hebrews 8:10-11 again.

Have the promises of the new covenant yet come to fruition in the lives of all of the people of Israel?

Has this process begun with some of the Jews and some of the Gentiles to date? How so?

When, exactly, did the new covenant begin? Read the following verses as you formulate your answer:

> Luke 16:16
>
> Mark 1:1
>
> Matthew 26:20-28
>
> Mark 14:22-24
>
> Luke 22:15-20

What evidences could one observe both 2000 years ago and now that the new covenant was and is operative in the lives of people?

Read Matthew 3:8-9 and comment.

Read Hebrews 8:12-13 again.

As part of this new covenant, how does God respond to the former sins of those who are following Him?

What makes it possible for Him to do this?

What happened to the old covenant and the Levitical priesthood when the new one came about?

Would you feel motivated to love God, worship God, and have a personal relationship with Him if your acceptance depended solely on animal sacrifices offered by a priest who was a stranger to you?

What would be the basis for this motivation?

Might you possibly get the incorrect impression that you were somehow manipulating God?

Application Questions

How much do biblical principles govern your thoughts and actions?

How can you use the truths in this passage to help a friend who is struggling to win approval from God by the works they perform?

Assignment for Next Session:

We need a volunteer to read and report on the book, *The Tabernacle: Shadows of the Messiah* by David M. Levy. We will accompany this report with a pamphlet on the tabernacle by Rose Publishing.

The Camp of Israel

In the first chapter of the book of Numbers, we find the numbering of the people of Israel.

While this seems somewhat inconsequential to the casual reader, we must remember that every detail of Scripture is there by design. We must then ask what in the world the Holy Spirit was trying to teach us by imparting what seems to be ancillary information.

While our understanding of this may be incomplete, we can make a number of very interesting and somewhat awe-inspiring observations.

First, from a historical point of view, it is important that one knows how many people were in the camp. However, we find more as we dig deeper.

The camp of Israel was always set up around the tabernacle. The tabernacle was cared for by the tribe of Levi. Moses, Aaron, and the priests camped on the east side next to the entrance. The three families of the tribe of Levi (Merari, Hohath, and Gershon) camped on the north, south, and west side, respectively. The remaining twelve tribes were camped around the tabernacle according to the very specific instructions given in the book of Numbers. (There were thirteen tribes, including the Levites.)

Each of the twelve tribes was clustered into one of four camps. Each of the groups was to rally to the standard of the lead tribe in the group. It is actually important from a symbolic and prophetic point of view to realize that the symbols of the lead tribes were as follows: the lion for Judah, the man for Reuben, the ox for Ephraim, and the eagle for Dan. These four symbols seem to be somewhat important at specific places in Scripture. They are the same as the four faces of the cherubim and we seem to encounter them in association with the throne of God. We can begin to see this in Ezekiel 1:10 and Revelation 4:7.

This leads us to our first discovery, which is that the camp of Israel, with the tabernacle in the center, seems to be a model of the throne of God.

In addition to this, when we go back to the numbering of the tribes in the camp of Israel as they were positioned around the tabernacle, we make further discoveries.

First, we need to realize that the total number of people in the camp was actually larger than the surface numbers mentioned, since only the men over twenty years of age and able to go to war were counted. If we multiply this number by a factor of three or four, we find that the camp may have held around two million individuals. Obviously, this was a really big camp.

When we try to visualize the camp, we first need to allow for the space required by the Levites in the center. If we allow for 100 yards, for instance, on each side for the Levites, that can then become the basic unit of width for the other camps. We assume this to be true since Scripture gives very specific details about the positioning of the other camps. Specifically, we find:

> The camp of Ephraim, comprising 108,100 fighting men and their families, extended directly to the west of the Levites.

> The camp of Judah, comprised of 186,400 fighting men and their families, extended directly to the east of the Levites.

> The camp of Dan, which was made up of 157,600 warriors and their families, extended directly to the north of the Levites.

> The camp of Ruben, which held 151,400 fighters and their families, extended directly to the south of the Levites.

We must note here that the four camps surrounding the Levites had the same width as the camp of the Levites and extended out directly only in the directions put forth in the Scriptures. No one was to be in the northeast, northwest, southeast, or southwest. Perhaps these areas were designated for other functions to be performed outside the camps (such as the establishment of latrines) as delineated in the Scriptures, but they were not part of the camps.

If we then diagram the camps that together make up the camp of Israel and draw them to scale, depending upon the number of people in each group, we make an amazing discovery. The camp of Israel was in the form of a cross!

Here we find an allusion in concrete terms to the coming Jewish Messiah, Yeshua Ha-Mashiach, known as Jesus Christ, long before His birth and resurrection.

This is yet another amazing example of the supernatural nature of the Word of God and His plan of redemption as it exists beyond the simple dimension of time as we know it.

W
Ephraim
108,100

S   Levi   N
Ruben   Dan
151,400   157,600

Judah
186,400
E

Close in prayer.

Review calendar.

Assign refreshments for next time.

WEEK 13

NOT TOO MUCH SUGAR, NOT TOO MUCH SPICE: JUST THE BEST COMBINATION TO GET EVERYTHING RIGHT

HEBREWS 9:1-10

Opening Prayer

The title of today's lesson gives us some insight into the passage we will be studying today. As we have said time and again, you can find Jesus Christ on every page of the Old Testament. Nowhere is this truer than in the construction of the tabernacle. Every detail of the structure has been supernaturally designed and points to the Jewish Messiah, Yeshua Ha-Mashiach, or Jesus Christ, when properly understood.

Properly understanding these concepts in their entirety, however, is a long and arduous undertaking. Many excellent books have been written on this topic alone. The discoveries one makes when coming to an understanding of these things are exciting almost beyond belief. They prove once again the supernatural nature of the documents we have before us.

Our goal today is to understand enough about this symbolism to get a sense of that supernatural excitement while at the same time finding lessons for our day-to-day lives.

Group Warm-Up Question

What religious customs do you, or other people with whom you are familiar, observe without really knowing why?

Read Hebrews 9:1-10

Read Hebrews 9:1-2 again.

What aspect of the old and new covenants is compared in this passage?

What was in the first room of the earthly tabernacle?

What was the first room called?

Read Hebrews 9:3-5 again.

What was behind the second curtain that stood before the entrance to the second room and what was it called?

What exactly was in this second room?

What was inside the Ark of the Covenant?

What was the significance of the various things inside the Ark of the Covenant?

What was spread over the top of the Ark of the Covenant?

What was the other name given to the cover of the Ark of the Covenant?

What was the significance of this?

Read Hebrews 9:5 again.

What important point does the writer make at the end of this verse?

Read Hebrews 9:6-7 again.

During the year who served at the tabernacle?

In what part of the tabernacle did this take place?

Who alone was permitted to go into the second part of the tabernacle?

What is the significance of this?

List the three very important severe restrictions placed upon this second room.

     1.

     2.

3.

What is the significance of these three important restrictions?

How do these three restrictions relate to Jesus Christ?

Read Hebrews 9:8-10 again.

What truths is the Holy Spirit overtly teaching us in these verses?

1.

2.

3.

4.

How are these limitations corrected, as noted in Hebrews 9:10?

Special Presentation: It is now our privilege to listen to a report on *The Tabernacle: Shadows of the Messiah* by David M. Levy. (As arranged previously) We will accompany this report with a pamphlet on the tabernacle by Rose Publishing.

We see that an understanding of the old covenant tabernacle is imperative as we again realize that the Word of God is an integrated message system. The whole of the tabernacle points to the new covenant in Jesus Christ. And we can also see that the tabernacle was inferior to what was coming in the new covenant for at least five specific reasons.

Five reasons the tabernacle and old covenant are inferior to the new covenant in Jesus Christ:

1. The tabernacle was an earthly sanctuary made by man.
   - Read Hebrews 9:11.
   - Read Hebrews 8:2.

2. The tabernacle was an earthly representation of something even greater.
   - Read Hebrews 9:23.

3. The tabernacle was inaccessible to the people on a personal basis.
   - Read Hebrews 9:6-7 again.
   - Read Hebrews 10:19 to see the contrast with the new covenant.

4. The tabernacle was temporary.
   - Read Hebrews 9:8 again.
   - Read Matthew 27:50-51 to see this change.

5. The tabernacle's ministry was external, not internal.
   - Read Hebrews 9:9-10 again.

Viewing the tabernacle, it appears that God dwells only in holy places. What does this say to us about our lives, minds and hearts?

How does Christ's sacrifice enable us to have a clear conscience?

Application Question

This passage should drive home God's holiness to us. How should this impact us on a day to day basis as we interact with God and read His Word?

Close in prayer.

Review calendar.

Assign refreshments for next time.

WEEK 14

FROM DEATH TO LIFE
HEBREWS 9:11-28

Opening Prayer

Group Warm-Up Question

What thoughts go through your mind and how do you feel as you contemplate your upcoming death?

Read Hebrews 9:11-28

Today the Scripture we are reviewing again deals with the tabernacle. You may be asking yourself why the author of Hebrews spent so much time on this subject. And you may also be asking yourself why we have spent a fair amount of time talking about it. We should remember that the tabernacle is mentioned in 50 of the 66 books of the Bible. This simple statistic is often overlooked like the tabernacle itself. God thinks the tabernacle is pretty important for us to read about again and again in His Word. If He thinks it is important for us to understand

125

and has great things to teach us, then we should also regard it with importance and learn from it.

Read Hebrews 9:11-13 again.

How is the tabernacle in which Jesus Christ serves as High Priest described?

How many times did Jesus Christ need to enter the most holy place?

How was the sacrifice of Jesus Christ different from the usual sacrifice on the Day of Atonement?

How was Jesus an unblemished sacrifice?

Read Hebrews 9:14 again.

This verse refers to actual deeds that result in death. Is this referring to spiritual death?

Under what circumstances might this be true?

In Hebrews 9:14, what benefits do we see believers realizing from the sacrifice Jesus made on their behalf?

How was it possible for the sacrifice of Christ to fully satisfy God's wrath over sin and to make us right with God?

Why could we not in any way receive our promised eternal inheritance apart from Christ?

I once listened to a presentation by a former leader of an international denomination about these deeds that result in death. He called his list a catalog of sin and it ran to 5 pages. As you think about such a list, ask yourself if this is the correct way to think about the subject.

Is it something that comes prior to a deed that causes one to go in the wrong direction?

Are we to be worried on a minute-by-minute basis that some behavior will send us to hell?

Or, conversely, are our hearts and minds to be such that our words, thoughts, and actions are pleasing to God on an automatic basis.

I have purposely avoided publishing my friend's list here. It is easy enough for anyone to think about the things they might include on such a document. Any of us could, I'm sure, using our own predelictions, construct such a list on our own.

Now read the following verses and discuss any list of deeds that "result in death" in the context of the whole of Scripture.

> Matthew 12:34-35
>
> Matthew 5:18-19
>
> Luke 7:21

Psalm 51:10

Hebrews 8:10

Romans 12:2

Philippians 4:4-9

2 Timothy 1:7

Read Hebrews 9:15 again.

What is the eternal inheritance promised to believers?

Read Hebrews 9:16-22 again.

What must happen for sins to be forgiven?

Read Hebrews 9:23-24 again.

Why did Christ need to enter heaven instead of simply going into an earthly manmade temple?

As we noted in our previous session and reviewed in our discussion of the tabernacle, every detail of the old system and the tabernacle itself is there by design. We don't have the time to go into all of the specifics of this in our session. However, an in-depth review of the book and charts we looked at the last time is an awe-inspiring and worthwhile endeavor. For today's session, we should at least reiterate the overriding basics of the significance of the details. In doing so, we would do well to review the following points:

The Importance of the Details

1. There is only one entrance to the tabernacle, which symbolically is Jesus Christ. Specifically relate Hebrews 9:11-12 to:

    Isaiah 53:2-5

    Isaiah 53:10-11

    Acts 4:12

2. The kinds of things we are discussing, including the relationship between the tabernacle and Jesus Christ are spiritually discerned. While one may come to the correct conclusions on an academic basis, they take on real meaning when coupled with insight borne of the Holy Spirit. Read:

    1 Corinthians 2:14

    2 Corinthians 4:4

3. The door can be only be specifically linked to Jesus Christ. Read:

    John 10:9

    John 10:1

4. There is one entrance, one door, one way, and that way is Jesus Christ. Read:

    John 14:6

Read Hebrews 9:25-26 again.

How is Jesus Christ absolutely and completely different from every other high priest?

Read Hebrews 9:27 again.

What fate awaits us all?

What extraordinary measures have some people taken to avoid this fate?

Why have some people gone to such extremes?

Read Hebrews 9:27-28 again.

Why do you think the author kept repeating that Christ's sacrifice was once and for all?

In what ways will Christ's second coming differ from the first?

How should the fact that we will all be judged impact the way we live?

Why do human beings sometimes stray from what they know is right, even in the face of this knowledge?

What can we do to prevent this and be sure that we live lives pleasing to God?

Read:

>   1 Thessalonians 5:16-24

>   Ephesians 3:17

>   Romans 8:9

>   Colossians 3:16

Application Question

In what concrete ways can you show your gratitude for what Jesus Christ has done for you?

Close in prayer.

Review calendar.

Assign refreshments for next time.

WEEK 15

Shadows from the Past Brought to Life
Hebrews 10:1-18

Opening Prayer

Group Warm-Up Question

What one thing would you be willing to buy at a very high price today if it meant you would always have all of it you needed, and would never have to pay for it again?

Read Hebrews 10:1-18

Read Hebrews 10:1 again.

When the writer spoke of the law, what did the Jewish believers reading his letter understand him to be talking about?

Jews would have spoken of the law as the Torah, which encompasses the first five books of Moses. This involves far more than what we find in Exodus 20. It incorporates all of Genesis, Exodus, Leviticus, Numbers, and Deuteronomy: the first five books of the Bible. To the Jews, these were the first five books of the then extant Scriptures, which they knew as the Tanakh and which Gentiles now call the Old Testament.

How is the law compared to the new covenant brought by Christ?

Read Hebrews 10:2 again.

If the sacrifices made under the law were able to make one perfect, would they have had to be repeated year after year?

Read Hebrews 10:3-4 again.

What functions did the animal sacrifices serve?

Another model is hinted at here, which is the acknowledgement of a debt for sin. The debt is not actually paid by the yearly sacrifices on Yom Kippur when sacrifices are made for sins, but the penalty is simply extended for another year, when sacrifices must again be offered.

Read Colossians 2:14

At that time in history, a certificate of debt was a penal, legal, or criminal term. When one was in jail, the jailer would actually keep this certificate of debt and mark off the years the criminal was in jail. If the prisoner escaped, the jailer was responsible for the years left on the prisoner's certificate of debt. When a criminal's debt was paid in full (all of his or her time had been served), the jailer would write the Greek word *tetelestai* on the certificate itself. This word, when translated, means "paid in full." This certificate then was the proof that the debt had been paid. When Paul talks about our certificate of debt, this is what people of the time thought about.

Read Romans 6:23.

What are the wages of sin?

When Jesus was on the cross, what were his last words?

Read John 19:30.

The Greek word translated "It is finished," which can also be translated as "paid in full," is *tetelestai*. This is exactly the same word printed on a certificate of debt. Jesus Christ was fully aware that He was paying the debt for our sin on an eternal basis.

Read Hebrews 10:5-9 again.

Read Isaiah 1:11-15.

Why were certain sacrifices offensive to God?

Why did God say that he would not listen to the prayers of some people as mentioned in Isaiah 1: 15?

Is it possible that while sacrifices offered improperly were offensive to God, sacrifices offered properly were actually a blessing to some people?

Read the following verses and comment:

> Leviticus 4:20

> Leviticus 4:26

> Leviticus 4:31

> Leviticus 4:35

This was actually a kind of judicial forgiveness and did not remove the guilt from people's hearts. If the diligent worshippers had been purged from sin once and for all, sacrifices would not have had to have been offered ever again. There was a desperate need for a better sacrifice because the blood of bulls and goats could not take away sins. It could only cover sin and postpone judgment.

If these Old Testament sacrifices for sin were not pleasing to God, why did He require them?

Did these sacrifices point forward to Jesus Christ?

Read Hebrews 10:7 again.

In addition, there is another Old Testament concept at work here.

Read Psalm 40:6-8.

To whom do you think the Psalmist was referring in Psalm 40:7-8?

The word used in Psalm 40:6 to describe ears being opened is actually referring the concept of becoming a bond slave by choice.

Read Exodus 21:1-6 to see how one became a bond slave in the Old Testament.

We see the following concepts linked through Hebrews, Psalms, and Exodus.

1. Doing God's will.
2. Having His law written upon one's heart.
3. Becoming a bond slave.

How does the combination of these concepts point forward to Jesus Christ?

As my friend Ron Jones so often says, if there is a concept or point of Scripture you are having trouble understanding, you can usually assume that the answer involves Jesus Christ and be right. Simply follow the admonishment in James 1:5 and put Jesus Christ in the center of it.

And just to top all of this off, Hebrews 10:7 and Psalm 40: 8 also seem to relate directly to the following verses. Please read these verses and comment:

Isaiah 50:4-6

John 4:34

John 5:30

John 6:38

John 17:4

It is simply amazing to see how the whole of Scripture interconnects and how our understanding is enhanced as we put it all together.

Read Hebrews 10:8-9 again.

Also read:

1 Samuel 15:22

Psalm 51:16-17

Isaiah 1:19

Hosea 6:6

What does it appear that God prefers over sacrifices?

Read Hebrews 10:10-14 again.

Read Colossians 2:10

What role does a believer play in earning God's approval?

What simple thing must a believer do?

What did Christ's single act of dying accomplish for those who would trust in Him?

Read Psalm 110:1

How do you relate this to Hebrews 10:13?

Read Hebrews 10:10 and Hebrews 10:14 again along with Romans 6: 22.

How does one put together the concept of having been made holy and at the same time being made holy?

Read Hebrews 10:15-16.

How can we know personally that we have this perfect standing before God?

When a believer appropriates this on a personal basis, what kinds of guilt feelings should they have or not have?

Read Hebrews 10:15-18 again.

Also read:

Hebrews 8:7-12

Jeremiah 31:33-34

How does the new covenant then change the way God motivates people to live for Him?

Application Question

What can you do this week to show trust in Christ's provision for your personal forgiveness?

Close in prayer.

Review calendar.

Assign refreshments for next time.

WEEK 16

SPECIFIC RECIPE FOR SUCCESS AND PERSEVERANCE
HEBREWS 10:19-39

Opening Prayer

Group Warm-Up Question

When in your life did you "hang in there" the longest in the face of what was an extremely difficult situation for you?

Read Hebrews 10:19-39

Read Hebrews 10:19-21 again.

Why did the author say those under the new covenant could draw near to God?

Specifically, what has Jesus done for those under the new covenant?

Read Hebrews 10:22-25 again.

These verses contain a lot of information. They do, in fact, provide a sort of a recipe for success. In them, we find four "let us" statements of great import. Please list them below:

1.

2.

3.

4.

Read Hebrews 10:22 again.

What must happen for one to truly enter the presence of God?

What privilege comes to those who have trusted Jesus Christ?

What happens to the guilty conscience of someone who puts their faith in Christ?

Where does this concept of having our consciences cleansed by being sprinkled with the blood of Christ come from?

Read the following verses for more insight into this subject:

    Exodus 24:8

    Leviticus 5:9

2 Chronicles 35:11

Hebrews 12:24

1 Peter 1:22

Here we see two important Levitical idioms. First, we see that we are to wash judicially in the Blood of Christ, which covers our sin. Second, we are to wash daily in the water of the Word. (The water is an idiom for the Word of God.) Read the following verses to get the flavor of the life-giving properties of God's Word likened to water:

Jeremiah 17:13

John 4:10-14

Ephesians 5:26

What important things should we remember about the effects of daily washing in the water of God's Word?

Read 2 Timothy 3:16-17.

Read Hebrews 10:23 again.

Why is it so important to hold tightly to our hope?

The use of the word "hope" in the Greek is the opposite of our use of the word in English. In the Greek, "hope" is a confidence, sureness, and knowledge of future things. In fact, in the Greek, the word "hope" infers a certainty stronger than knowing. It is an ultimate, internal, overpowering, all-enveloping eternal surety and truth that is absolute.

Read Hebrews 10:24-25 again.

What happens when we are obedient in following the directives to encourage and warn one another?

What happens when believers are not obedient in encouraging and warning one another?

Why is it so important that believers meet together on a regular basis?

What happens to believers if they do not meet together on a regular basis?

Why do you think the writer says that meeting together becomes even more important as the day of His coming back draws near?

Read Hebrews 10:26-31 again.

What will happen to God's enemies?

What was the penalty in the Old Testament for refusing to obey the law of Moses?

Read Hebrews 10:29 again.

Why is it so much worse to treat the blood of the covenant as common and unholy, thereby effectively trampling the Son of God under foot?

What is the import of enraging the Holy Spirit?

The term used for the Holy Spirit in Hebrews 10:29 is used in only one other place in Scripture. That is in Zechariah 12:10. In the King James Version, this is translated "the Spirit of Grace."

What, in your opinion, is the importance of this?

What exactly is happening when someone does this?

Is this rejecting of Jesus Christ and thereby enraging and blaspheming the Holy Spirit what is known as the unforgivable sin?

Read Mark 3:28-29 and comment.

Read Hebrews 10:30 again, then look at the following verses and discuss this concept:

   Deuteronomy 32:35

   Deuteronomy 32:36-37

   Romans 12:19

Read Hebrews 10:32-34 again.

What kinds of things happened to these Hebrew Christians as a result of their faith in Jesus Christ?

How had the Hebrew Christians to whom this letter was written first responded to the terrible persecution they endured?

Read Hebrews 10:35-39 again.

What were these early Jewish believers being exhorted to do in their then current dire circumstances?

Having lost everything in this world, why would any of these Jewish believers even be tempted to give up when they had an eternal biblical hope? (Review the concept of biblical hope.)

Why do believers today sometimes have ups and downs in their spiritual lives?

How does this relate back to the prescription in the four "let us" statements we found in Hebrews 10:22-25?

How do these concepts interrelate with the following verses?

    Habakkuk 2:4

    Romans 1:17

    Galatians 3:11

Hebrews 10:38

Luke 9:62

John 10:28-29

How then do the concepts of faith, a biblical hope, and Jesus' statement of fact in John 10:28-29 work together?

How could a believing friend help to spur you on "toward love and good deeds?"

Application Questions

What one small thing can you do this week to encourage a believing friend in their faith?

Close in prayer.

Review calendar.

Assign refreshments for next time.

WEEK 17

WE LIVE BY FAITH
HEBREWS 11:1-40

Opening Prayer

Group Warm-Up Question

If you were to listen to your own funeral service, what would you like to hear them say about you?

Read Hebrews 11:1-40

What is faith?

What does faith help us to understand about the creation of the universe?

Read John 1:1-3 and discuss how it relates to the statement about creation in Hebrews.

Read Hebrews 11:2 again.

Why do you think God puts such a high premium on being believed?

Read Hebrews 11:3 again.

What allusion to things that modern man has discovered through science is made in this verse?

Modern science has discovered that everything seems to be made up of small invisible particles called molecules. Molecules are made up of atoms. Atoms are essentially highly energetic particles quite distant from one another in relative terms, but having the ability to interact with other things by virtue of their unseen electrical fields.

You may remember the Bohr model of the atom from high school. The center or nucleus of an atom is made up of neutrons (particles with a neutral charge) and protons (positively charged particles) and is surrounded by negatively charged particles called electrons which "orbit" around the nucleus.

Atoms can have different combinations of neutrons, protons, and electrons. The different combination of these minute particles is what makes up the basic elements listed on what we call the periodic table.

The great mystery that scientists cannot explain is what holds the nucleus of an atom together. It should, by its very nature, come apart. However, students of the Bible understand what does indeed hold the atom as well as the whole universe together.

Read Colossians 1:15-17 for more information on this topic.

An interesting adjunct to this is found in Revelation 21. Take a moment and read this passage. Did anything jump out at you as being different than you might expect?

Reread Revelation 21 and pay particular attention to verses 18 and 21. Most readers, upon reading that the gold was "as clear as glass," simply skip over the phrase and ignore it. However, "modern" science tells us that gold in the most refined form is indeed as clear as glass. This form of gold is used in high level telecommunications equipment where maximum conductivity is required. One would not use it in Jewelry, where the traditional colors springing from impurities in the metal are desired. Indeed, in one of our study sessions, Scott Swart, a former Marine with a White House security clearance, told us how he personally saw gold on very advanced electronic equipment in a highly refined state when in the military. It was clear, albeit a little smoky. Further refinement reportedly makes it just as referenced in Revelation.

Perhaps just as interesting is that John, the writer of Revelation, was simply writing down what he heard and saw. He had no idea what "modern science" would tell us about gold. He just reported the facts. As with the rest of God's Word, this particular fact was simply corroborated later when our ability to understand things caught up to the reality revealed in the Scriptures.

This instance, like all others of the same nature, should simply serve to put us more in awe of the Word of God and help us to realize its supernatural nature.

Read Hebrews 11:4 again.

How did Abel demonstrate his faith and what was the result?

Read Hebrews 11:5 again.

What was the result of Enoch's faith?

Read Hebrews 11:6 again.

How does faith relate to coming to God and pleasing Him?

What is the only way we can please God with our lives?

Read Hebrews 11:7 again.

Noah was a real person. What was the result of his faith?

Read Hebrews 11:8-12 again.

Also read Genesis 12:1-4.

How did Abraham's faith impact his life?

How did Abraham's faith impact the lives of others?

Specifically, who else benefited from his faith?

Read Hebrews 11:10 again.

This says that Abraham was looking for an eternal city.

In the Old Testament, we read that Abraham named the place where he went to sacrifice Isaac "Jehovah-Jireh" or "Jireh-shalom," the root for Jerusalem. This is somewhat remarkable when we investigate the meaning of these Hebrew words. "Jehovah" is God, "Jireh" means provides or provider, and as most everyone knows "shalom" means peace. What most people do not realize, however, is that in the Hebrew *shalom* also infers completeness and wholeness. When we put this together we get "Jehovah provides completeness and wholeness through His peace." What a wonderful prophetic picture this is of Jesus Christ and his sacrifice that would provide the ultimate in inner peace, wholeness, and completion as we see in John 14: 6.

We learn more about this holy and eternal city in Revelation 21. Read this passage to gain a better understanding of what Abraham looked forward to.

Here we see an event occurring thousands of years ago tied to an event yet to come in history. Somehow, through the inspiration of the Holy Spirit, Abraham spoke about the coming New Jerusalem when it had not yet been written about in any detail. This is another one of those times when the supernatural nature of the Scriptures is so evident that it might send shivers up and down your spine.

Read Hebrews 11:13-16 again.

In what ways does faith change a person's focus and perspective on life? List as many as you can.

Read Hebrews 11:17-19 again.

What additional great test of faith did Abraham have in his life?

What was necessary for Abraham to please God when his faith was tested?

What is necessary for us to please God when faced with a difficult situation?

Read Hebrews 11:22 again.

How sure was Joseph in his confidence in the promise of God to bring the Israelites out of Egypt?

Was this confidence warranted?

Read the following verses to see this playing out.

> Genesis 50:25
>
> Exodus 13:19
>
> Joshua 24:32

Read Hebrews 11:23-28 again.

What difficult choices did Moses make because of his faith?

What made it possible for Moses to make these choices?

Does this same principle apply to us in our lives when we are faced with difficult choices and situations?

What great advantage do we have over Moses when faced with hard times in life? What resource do we have that he did not have?

Read Romans 10:17 and comment.

Read Hebrews 11:29 again.

Here we find an interesting lesson about faith properly placed in God versus a belief sincerely held.

The Israelites were safe as they passed through the Red Sea because of their faith in God.

The Egyptians drowned while trying to pass through the sea because they sincerely believed that if a path remained open for the Jews, it would also enable them to pass through.

In the world today, sometimes even in the church, people tend to think that a belief sincerely held will make them okay, even if they are wrong in the belief. Their sincerity is accorded a higher value by such people and by our society than is the truth.

What is wrong with this faith in sincerity and how should we respond to it?

Read Hebrews 11:30-34 again.

What great victories did these Old Testament believers enjoy because of their faith?

Read Hebrews 11:35-38 again.

What difficulties did other Old Testament believers experience because of their faith?

Read Hebrews 11:39-40 again.

What one thing did the Old Testament believers mentioned in Hebrews 11:32-38 have in common?

Is it accurate to say that all the believers mentioned were victorious in eternal terms?

Read the following verses and comment.

> 1 John 5:4
>
> 1 Corinthians 15:50-58

Application Questions

What specific thing do you need to take to God in faith and trust Him with today?

How can you show that you have trusted God in this matter?

Close in prayer.

Review calendar.

Assign refreshments for next time.

WEEK 18

DISCIPLINE IN THE LIVES
OF TRUE BELIEVERS
HEBREWS 12:1-13

Opening Prayer

Group Warm-Up Question

When in your life did you endure difficult circumstances because you expected that you would be rewarded later on?

Read Hebrews 12:1-13

Read Hebrews 12:1 again.

Who is involved in this "great cloud of witnesses?"

What does it mean that we are "compassed about" or "surrounded" by them?

What warning do we find in this verse?

Why does sin so easily hinder us?

The imagery in this verse comes from athletics. The Greek word used for weight means "fat" in Greek. What is this "fat" that can slow us down?

Read 1 Corinthians 9:24-27

How does this relate to the concepts in Hebrews 12:1?

Read Hebrews 12:2 again.

In our world, having faith is often spoken of with relatively high regard. This is often couched in terms of the personal faith that one has. It is not uncommon to hear someone say that they have a "deep and personal" faith when asked about their religious affiliation or their trust in God. How does this "deep and personal faith" contrast or compare with what we read in this verse?

Read the following verses and discuss how they relate to Jesus Christ.

> Isaiah 8:17
>
> Numbers 21:4-9
>
> John 3:14-16

Read Matthew 14:22-33.

What happens when we take our eyes off of Jesus?

Read Hebrews 12:2 again.

This verse also says that Jesus knew that he would die on the cross and afterward experience joy and the highest honor possible.

Read the following verses and discuss how we see this spoken of beforehand, and what result we see from it today:

> Psalm 16:8-10
>
> Psalm 110:1
>
> Psalm 110:4
>
> Acts 2:34-36
>
> Hebrews 10:12
>
> Jude 24

Read Hebrews 12:3-4 again.

Read John 17:4.

Jesus endured humanly unimaginable things on our behalf, including death, which we can imagine.

Do believers in the world today often endure death because of their faith in Jesus Christ?

In the United States, most believers have become too complacent about their faith. The Voice of the Martyrs tells us that every year 150,000 believers in Jesus Christ are murdered for their faith. This breaks down to 411 per day, or 17 each hour. These brothers and sisters do not normally receive a clean death. They are most often subjected to starvation, torture, rape, and deprivation of the worst kind.

Are you prepared to endure to the end, even if it means dying for your faith?

As you contemplate this question consider the following:

1. In discussing the concept of enduring to the end with Rabbi Kipp he pointed out the necessity of living in the positive and daily expectation of the return of the Jewish Messiah, Yeshua Ha-Maschiach, who we know as Jesus.

2. In discussing this with a believing lawyer they wondered if perhaps one might give a lawyerly answer that seemed to deny one's faith in order to prolong their earthly life one more day. After all, they said, God would know you weren't serious about it. You would just be kidding. (As they say down south in the USA, "that dog just won't hunt.")

3. As of this writing there is a believer in Iran imprisoned for his faith in a very public trial. He has the choice of denying Jesus Christ and living or declaring his allegiance to Him and dying. He has chosen to remain true to his Lord. (For a believer there really is no other choice.)

Read the following verses and discuss them in the context of enduring to the end:

> Mark 13: 13
>
> Matthew 10: 28
>
> Matthew 10: 32-33

Read Hebrews 12:5-8 again.

In verse 5, the author speaks about an important thing his readers seem to have forgotten. We also see this highlighted in Hebrews 5:11-12. What vitally important thing were these believers neglecting?

How can we as believers prevent this from happening to us today? Please list as many things as you can.

The Greek word used in Hebrews 12:5-8 for chastening or disciplining relates to "training one's child, discipline, and instruction." However, this is not just directed to new believers. It is important to note that the Greek word translated sons (KJV), and in some versions rendered "children," refers to adult sons in the original language.

Read the following passages to see some of the implications of this standing as adult children of God.

> Romans 8:14-18
>
> Galatians 4:1-7

Read the following verses to learn more about the privilege of being chastened as a true child of God.

Proverbs 3:11

Proverbs 3:12

Job 5:17

Psalm 94:12

1 Peter 4:12-17

Is it possible that God can use even the attacks of our enemies to discipline us and help us grow?

Read Hebrews 12:8 again.

What sobering truth can be inferred by those who never experience the discipline of God?

Read Hebrews 12:9-11 again.

Why does God discipline His children?

What is the result of this discipline?

Read Hebrews 12:12-13 again, and also read the following verses:

> 1 Timothy 4:7-8

> Isaiah 35:3

> Proverbs 4:26

What admonitions for our lives do we find in these verses?

To whom is the text referring when it speaks of "those who follow after us?"

What promises do we find for those who follow after us if we follow the admonitions of Scripture that we just read?

Why do you think those who follow after us will "not stumble and become strong" if we respond properly to God's discipline in our lives?

Application Questions

How can you help your friends who have placed their personal trust in Jesus Christ persevere as believers by what you do and say this week?

How can you call on your believing friends to help you persevere as a follower of Jesus Christ?

Close in prayer.

Review calendar.

Assign refreshments for next time.

WEEK 19

ENCOURAGEMENT AND WARNING
HEBREWS 12:14-29

Opening Prayer

Group Warm-Up Question

What are some warnings in life that you have received and been grateful for?

Read Hebrews 12:14-29

Read Hebrews 12:14 again.

Believers are told to pursue holiness. What exactly does this mean?

The American Heritage Deluxe dictionary defines being holy as "being like God or in the service of or worship of God."

What (or who) is the best example we as human beings have had of what this means?

Read the following verses and comment:

> 1 Thessalonians 4: 1-7

> 1 Peter 1:15

Why is this so important?

What roadblocks can make it difficult for someone to pursue holiness?

Read the following verses to learn more about the holiness that God expects to see in our lives.

> 1 Peter 1:15

> 1 Peter 1:16

> 1 Peter 2:5

> 1 Peter 2:9

> 2 Peter 3:11

Read Hebrews 12:15 again.

What wrong attitude do believers need to watch out for?

Humanly speaking, why is it so easy for people to develop this negative attitude?

What are the results in a person's life when they develop this negative attitude?

Read Hebrews 12:16-17 again.

What wrong attitude did Esau develop?

To what actions did Esau's wrong attitude lead?

What was the ultimate result of Esau's wrong attitude and actions?

Read Hebrews 12:18-21 again.

In what ways might the old covenant have been intimidating or frightening to people?

What do we learn about the character of God in Hebrews 12:18-21?

Read Hebrews 12:22-24 again.

These verses list a number of things that we have come to under the new covenant. Please list these things. There are at least seven.

1.

2.

3.

4.

5.

6.

7.

Read Hebrews 12:25 again.

What admonition do we find in this verse?

How is God speaking to us?

What terrible danger must we avoid?

Read Hebrews 12:26-27 again.

In what ways were the pronouncements of God from Mount Sinai a foreshadowing of things yet to come?

Was the author of Hebrews the first one to write about this? Read Haggai 2:6 and find out.

Read Hebrews 12:28-29 again.

How should God's promises and the reality of His kingdom affect believers?

How should this impact the way we worship God?

Application Question

What steps do you need to take this week to prevent becoming bitter toward someone who has hurt you? (Remember Esau.)

Close in prayer.

Review calendar.

Assign refreshments for next week.

WEEK 20

Opening Prayer

Group Warm-Up Question

What one thing would you want to say to your loved ones if you could write them a last letter or somehow leave a videotaped message behind for them?

Read Hebrews 13:1-25

The first nine verses of Chapter 13 speak of continuing in love. The most interesting part of these nine verses is that they seem to further dissect love into seven subdivisions and evidences of love. (Remember the significance of the number seven in Scripture.)

Read Hebrews 13:1-9 again.
As you read through these verses, stop as indicated below and discuss how the noted verse relates to the topic put forth.

EVIDENCE #1: HOSPITALITY

Read Hebrews 13:2 again, then read Romans 12:13.

What does this say to us about love showing itself through hospitality? (The writer refers specifically to what happened to Abraham in Genesis 18.)

In the Middle East today, especially in the absence of places to stay for travelers, hospitality is regarded as a sacred duty.

In Paul's day, hospitality meant putting up travelers, without charge, in one's home while they were in town. The travelers would normally carry letters of introduction from people trusted by their hosts, attesting that they were to be accepted as guests.

Neither they, nor we, were told to take this mindlessly out of context.

EVIDENCE #2: SYMPATHY

Read Hebrews 13:3 again.

What aspect of love is shown through sympathy and empathy?

This verse is often taken out of context as an exhortation to engage in prison ministry to every person who is incarcerated. While a prison ministry is a wonderful thing, it is more associated with what we commonly call "the Great Commission" than with this verse. At the time this was written to the Hebrews, members of their own fellowship and faith were being imprisoned for their faith and faithfulness to Jesus Christ. (See also Hebrews 13:23 in this same passage.) This was, at that time, a call to remember their fellow believers.

EVIDENCE #3: UNFLINCHING PERSONAL PURITY

Read Hebrews 13:4 again.

How is continuing in love evidenced in our personal purity and faithfulness in marriage?

Does this mean that one who is not faithful is not continuing to evidence the love commanded in the Scriptures?

EVIDENCE #4: CONTENTMENT IN ALL CIRCUMSTANCES

Read Hebrews 13:5 again.

Read Romans 8:28-39 for an expansion of this concept.

How does contentment and having a proper view of money evidence love in our lives?

Warren Wiersbe tells a story about a Christian couple who was traveling behind what was called the "Iron Curtain" in Eastern Europe. They were taking blankets, Bibles, Christian literature, and many personal necessities to the believers living in situations of great deprivation. This couple assured these persecuted believers that Christians in America were praying for them.

However, one of the persecuted and suffering believers replied by saying "We are happy for that, but we feel that Christians in America need more prayer than we do. We here in Eastern Europe are suffering, but you in America are very comfortable; and it is always harder to be a good Christian when you are comfortable."

What do you make of this story and what the persecuted believer had to say?

EVIDENCE #5: COMPLETE CONFIDENCE

Read Hebrews 13:6 again.

Read Psalm 118:6.

How does having this biblical confidence show God's love in our lives?

EVIDENCE #6: PRAYER FOR OTHERS

Read Hebrews 13:7 again.

How is love shown when we pray for leaders in our family of believers?

EVIDENCE #7: STABILITY AND PROPER BIBLICAL DOCTRINE

Read Hebrews 13:8-9 again.

How is love shown in our lives when we remain faithful to Jesus Christ and the Word of God?

Why is it important for us to remember that Jesus Christ is the same yesterday, today, and forever?

The points made in Hebrews 13:8-9 are very important. Read and discuss the following verses to see how they tie into the same concept in some other places in Scripture:

2 Peter 2:1-3

Matthew 7:15

Matthew 7:21-32

Mark 13:22-23

It is also instructive to note that Hebrews 13:8-9 does not say that the "strange doctrines" it references are in every instance technically untrue. They are simply not profitable for us to narrowly focus upon and are certainly not the source of our strength, which comes to us through Jesus Christ by the grace of God. The example the writer uses here has to do with ceremonial foods.

Might certain areas of concentrated biblical study also result in a believer being thrown off track if one loses sight of the object and purpose of our faith?

Might this concentration on certain topics to the exclusion of a personal relationship with the ultimate Author of our faith befall even ministers or seminary professors?

In preparing the study of Hebrews, I was faced with just such a question when dealing with the subjects of Melchizedek and Christophanies. It seemed apparent after studying the Scriptures that Melchizedek was a real person being referenced as an example or type of Christ.

 I then thought that perhaps I should include a chapter on Christophanies. As I began this work, I defined the characteristics of such an event and what might qualify an event to be considered an Old Testament appearance of Jesus. Doing this was very interesting. Amazingly, I found a great number of things in the Tanakh that might qualify to be included in this category. Each one, of course, might lead to a great deal of further discussion.

However, discussing this topic becomes almost inane even when one discusses it with great scholarship. Whether or not any particular event in the Old Testament is a Christophany can be helpful as a part of any discussion of the Scripture in question. However, if one concentrates too intently and exclusively on this topic, it throws you off track from the ultimate goal of our faith. While I may be absolutely convinced about the correctness of my position in regard to Melchizedek, and am happy to discuss it, neither my faith nor that of anyone else hinges upon this issue.

Therefore, although it became apparent to me that one might write a very long, very scholarly, and probably very boring book about this subject, I decided to forego the temptation to include a chapter dealing specifically with Christophanies. Instead, I simply presented Melchizedek as the Scriptures present him, which is as a type of Christ. As I prayed for wisdom about this, delving into the subject too deeply seemed unprofitable for both me and those who may utilize this study. After all, the goal of these studies is to help believers understand and enjoy the Scriptures as they apply them to their lives and experience the exhilarating and unspeakable privilege of a personal relationship with God through the person of Jesus Christ and the indwelling of the Holy Spirit.

This might seem a long explanation. But believe me, it is more interesting and profitable than slogging through page after page of analysis and discussion of Christophanies.

Read Hebrews 13:10 again.

At the time this was written, there was no altar, nor was there a temple in which sacrifices could be made for sins. The author is reminding us about what we learned in Hebrews 9 and 10. There we were clearly led to understand that Jesus Christ presented Himself in a heavenly tabernacle and that His sacrifice is and was effective as a sacrifice for our sins.

Read Hebrews 13:11-12 again, then read:

> Leviticus 4:11-12
>
> Leviticus 4:21

How was Jesus' crucifixion outside the gates of the city a fulfillment of Old Testament law regarding sacrifices?

How was what Jesus did outside the gates so much more significant and superior to the sacrifice of the priests outside the camp spoken of in Leviticus?

Read Hebrews 13:13-14 again.

Remember that this letter was written to Hebrew believers who were tempted to return to the legalism of Judaism. They are here being encouraged to be sure to leave the legalistic system of Judaism and graduate and cling to the freedom they have found in Yeshua Ha-Mashiach, Jesus Christ, the Jewish Messiah.

They are *not* being told to leave their Jewish heritage. They are being told to leave behind a dead religion in lieu of a personal relationship with Jesus Christ. Anyone can enjoy and participate in a religious service or organization. Only a regenerated person can properly worship the Living God and participate in a relationship with him through Jesus Christ and the indwelling of the Holy Spirit.

Do non-Jews today suffer from the same type of problems and temptations to engage in dead religious practices faced by the Jews referenced in Hebrews? How so?

Read Hebrews 13:15-16 again.

What sacrifices are we told to offer today?

How are these sacrifices superior to the blood of animals on an altar?

What impact do these sacrifices have on the recipient?

On the one making the sacrifice?

On God?

Read Hebrews 13:17 again.

What is to be our relationship to our spiritual leaders?

What qualities should we seek in those whom we accept as spiritual leaders?

Read 1 Timothy 3:1-13 for an excellent summary of these qualities. Please list them here. You should be able to come up with about twenty.

Why must we always be sure to remember to focus on our personal relationship with God as well as the Scriptures, even while relating to our spiritual leaders?

Read Hebrews 13:18-19 again.

Why was it important that so intelligent and godly a person as the author of Hebrews ask for and receive the prayer support of those he was writing to?

What does this teach us about humility?

Read Hebrews 13:20-21 again.

How do these verses coincide with what we read in Colossians 3:23-24?

Read Hebrews 13:22 again.

Why was it so vital that the Jewish believers to whom this letter was written pay close attention to it?

Read Hebrews 13:23-25 again.

Many people take these three verses to be the final proof that Paul wrote the book of Hebrews. In verse 23, the writer says he is hoping to come to visit with Timothy, who was recently released from jail after being incarcerated for his faith. This certainly sounds like Paul.

In verse 24, we see a reference to the believers in Italy. Many scholars believe this is reference to the believers in Rome and they further believe that Paul wrote this letter from that city.

In verse 25, the writer closes by saying:

> 25 May God's grace be with you all. (NLT)

> 25 Grace be with you all. Amen. (KJV)

This can also be found in the epistles from Paul. Some call it his "secret mark."

While this is interesting, it goes into the same category as the Christophanies. Too much concentration on this question becomes an exercise in academic nonsense. Some day we will all know which human being God used to bring the book of Hebrews to us. What is vitally important, however, is that we all know the Author of all Scripture on an intimate, effective, and personal basis.

When we began the study on this passage, we asked what final message you would leave behind for loved ones. This is actually a very important thing for each of us to consider. Strange as it may seem, people often listen more closely to a "voice from the grave" than they do to someone sitting beside them.

Application Questions

What action steps can you take now to make the creation of such a message for those you love a reality?

Note: Whatever the steps are for each of us, we need to follow up and do it, not just talk about doing it.

Which believing friend or friends can you encourage to continue walking in their relationship with Christ on a daily basis?

How will you do it?

Close in prayer.

Review calendar.

Assign refreshments for next time.

CPSIA information can be obtained at www.ICGtesting.com
Printed in the USA
LVOW03s0725260914

405895LV00002B/2/P